# Zoom Hog Bi

| | | | | |
|---|---|---|---|---|
| "Asks for input after everyone has already shared." | "Doesn't realize their camera is on." | "Argues over the meeting's purpose." | "Turns the camera off without explanation." | "Talks about their workout routine." |
| "Refers to an email no one has seen." | "Says 'I'll just follow up later.'" | Free | "Says 'This is off-topic, but...'" | "Blames their tech issues on the software." |
| "Asks for slides mid-meeting." | "Has kids running in the background." | "Complains about the meeting length." | "Asks to 'circle back to that later.'" | "Says 'Can we take a quick break?'" |
| "Says 'Can I play devil's advocate?'" | "Says 'Can we revisit this next week?'" | "Talks with their mouth full." | "Complains about meeting fatigue." | "Shares an unrequested opinion." |
| "Forgets to turn their mic off after the meeting ends." | "Gets frustrated about a tech issue." | "Interrupts the host to go back to their point." | "Describes their home office setup." | "Says 'Let's workshop this.'" |

Name: _____

Date of meeting: _____

# Zoom Hog Bingo!

| | | | | |
|---|---|---|---|---|
| "Says 'Let's put a pin in this.'" | "Explains the same point three different ways." | "Talks about their weekend in detail." | "Starts a sentence with 'In my experience...'" | "Asks to reschedule partway through." |
| "Says 'I'm not sure this is relevant, but...'" | "Laughs awkwardly after a bad joke." | "Says 'Just to piggyback on that...'" | "Asks for everyone's opinion on a minor issue." | "Rants about a minor issue." |
| "Gets frustrated about a tech issue." | "Leaves their mic on during private conversation." | "Requests the host to extend the meeting." | "Has their pet make a cameo on-screen." | "Mentions how much coffee they've had." |
| "Uses the phrase 'going forward.'" | "Uses jargon no one understands." | "Tells a story no one asked for." | "Requests to 'table this discussion.'" | "Keeps asking for more examples." |
| "Says 'Can you email me the notes?'" | Free | "Uses 'at the end of the day' excessively." | "Forgets they're muted when starting a long sentence." | "Complains about their kids being noisy." |

Name: _____

Date of meeting: _____

# Zoom Hog Bingo!

| | | | | |
|---|---|---|---|---|
| "Complains about the time of the meeting." | "Gives an overly detailed update." | "Says 'Can we take a step back for a second?'" | "Says 'Can you repeat that last part?'" | "Keeps calling the host by the wrong name." |
| "Says 'This is a silly question, but...'" | "Takes a phone call during the meeting." | "Asks 'Is everyone still here?'" | "Takes the discussion way off-topic." | "Forgets to share their screen properly." |
| "Suggests splitting into another meeting." | "Asks if everyone can see their screen." | "Asks for a topic to be discussed again." | "Uses a fun filter, like cat ears." | "Mutes and unmutes repeatedly." |
| "Clicks their pen loudly." | "Requests to stay longer after the meeting ends." | "Mentions the weather." | "Tries to explain technical issues in detail." | "Eats loudly during the call." |
| "Mentions their upcoming vacation." | "Talks about a personal problem." | "Loses their train of thought mid-sentence." | Free | "Says 'Let me circle back to that.'" |

Name: _____

Date of meeting: _____

# Zoom Hog Bingo!

| | | | | |
|---|---|---|---|---|
| "Asks if this meeting is being recorded." | "Says 'I'll email you later about this.'" | "Talks to someone off-screen during the call." | "Claims they didn't get the agenda." | "Repeats the same question multiple times." |
| "Talks about lunch plans." | "Mentions how tired they are." | "Complains about their camera not working." | "Explains something already covered." | "Joins from their car." |
| "Interrupts to say 'Let me rephrase that.'" | "Mentions their bad internet connection." | "Shares their screen without warning." | Free | "Uses a distracting virtual background." |
| "Uses 'umm' excessively." | "Says 'This will only take a minute.'" | "Mentions how busy they are." | "Starts with 'This might be a stupid question, but...'" | "Talks over the host." |
| "Has loud background noise." | "Cracks an awkward joke that no one laughs at." | "Turns off their camera mid-meeting." | "Asks for a poll to be done." | "Overexplains their point." |

Name: _____

Date of meeting: _____

# Zoom Hog Bingo!

| | | | | |
|---|---|---|---|---|
| "Mentions their weekend plans." | "Says 'Just one more question.'" | "Suggests scheduling a follow-up meeting." | "Forgets to unmute before talking." | "Complains about technical difficulties." |
| "I know we're over time, but..." | Free | "Uses the word 'synergy' or 'circle back.'" | "Sorry, I didn't catch that—can you repeat it?" | "Thanks everyone at least three times." |
| "Let me just add one quick point." | "Talks about something unrelated to work." | "Asks for the slides or notes to be sent after the meeting." | "Repeats what someone else just said." | "Interrupts the speaker to make a point." |
| "Says 'Can everyone hear me?'" | "Joins late and asks to recap everything." | "Mentions their pet or child during the call." | "Asks a question unrelated to the topic." | "Talks over someone else." |
| "Goes on a long personal anecdote." | "Keeps their camera off and only chimes in to talk." | "Says 'I'll keep this brief' but doesn't." | "Can we circle back to what I said earlier?" | "Asks for clarification after it was explained." |

Name: _____

Date of meeting: _____

# Zoom Hog Bingo!

| | | | | |
|---|---|---|---|---|
| "Asks for input after everyone has already shared." | "Doesn't realize their camera is on." | "Argues over the meeting's purpose." | "Turns the camera off without explanation." | "Talks about their workout routine." |
| "Refers to an email no one has seen." | "Says 'I'll just follow up later.'" | Free | "Says 'This is off-topic, but...'" | "Blames their tech issues on the software." |
| "Asks for slides mid-meeting." | "Has kids running in the background." | "Complains about the meeting length." | "Asks to 'circle back to that later.'" | "Says 'Can we take a quick break?'" |
| "Says 'Can I play devil's advocate?'" | "Says 'Can we revisit this next week?'" | "Talks with their mouth full." | "Complains about meeting fatigue." | "Shares an unrequested opinion." |
| "Forgets to turn their mic off after the meeting ends." | "Gets frustrated about a tech issue." | "Interrupts the host to go back to their point." | "Describes their home office setup." | "Says 'Let's workshop this.'" |

Name: _____

Date of meeting: _____

# Zoom Hog Bingo!

| | | | | |
|---|---|---|---|---|
| "Says 'Let's put a pin in this.'" | "Explains the same point three different ways." | "Talks about their weekend in detail." | "Starts a sentence with 'In my experience...'" | "Asks to reschedule partway through." |
| "Says 'I'm not sure this is relevant, but...'" | "Laughs awkwardly after a bad joke." | "Says 'Just to piggyback on that...'" | "Asks for everyone's opinion on a minor issue." | "Rants about a minor issue." |
| "Gets frustrated about a tech issue." | "Leaves their mic on during private conversation." | "Requests the host to extend the meeting." | "Has their pet make a cameo on-screen." | "Mentions how much coffee they've had." |
| "Uses the phrase 'going forward.'" | "Uses jargon no one understands." | "Tells a story no one asked for." | "Requests to 'table this discussion.'" | "Keeps asking for more examples." |
| "Says 'Can you email me the notes?'" | Free | "Uses 'at the end of the day' excessively." | "Forgets they're muted when starting a long sentence." | "Complains about their kids being noisy." |

Name: _____

Date of meeting: _____

# Zoom Hog Bingo!

| | | | | |
|---|---|---|---|---|
| "Complains about the time of the meeting." | "Gives an overly detailed update." | "Says 'Can we take a step back for a second?'" | "Says 'Can you repeat that last part?'" | "Keeps calling the host by the wrong name." |
| "Says 'This is a silly question, but...'" | "Takes a phone call during the meeting." | "Asks 'Is everyone still here?'" | "Takes the discussion way off-topic." | "Forgets to share their screen properly." |
| "Suggests splitting into another meeting." | "Asks if everyone can see their screen." | "Asks for a topic to be discussed again." | "Uses a fun filter, like cat ears." | "Mutes and unmutes repeatedly." |
| "Clicks their pen loudly." | "Requests to stay longer after the meeting ends." | "Mentions the weather." | "Tries to explain technical issues in detail." | "Eats loudly during the call." |
| "Mentions their upcoming vacation." | "Talks about a personal problem." | "Loses their train of thought mid-sentence." | Free | "Says 'Let me circle back to that.'" |

Name: _____

Date of meeting: _____

# Zoom Hog Bingo!

| | | | | |
|---|---|---|---|---|
| "Asks if this meeting is being recorded." | "Says 'I'll email you later about this.'" | "Talks to someone off-screen during the call." | "Claims they didn't get the agenda." | "Repeats the same question multiple times." |
| "Talks about lunch plans." | "Mentions how tired they are." | "Complains about their camera not working." | "Explains something already covered." | "Joins from their car." |
| "Interrupts to say 'Let me rephrase that.'" | "Mentions their bad internet connection." | "Shares their screen without warning." | Free | "Uses a distracting virtual background." |
| "Uses 'umm' excessively." | "Says 'This will only take a minute.'" | "Mentions how busy they are." | "Starts with 'This might be a stupid question, but...'" | "Talks over the host." |
| "Has loud background noise." | "Cracks an awkward joke that no one laughs at." | "Turns off their camera mid-meeting." | "Asks for a poll to be done." | "Overexplains their point." |

Name: _____

Date of meeting: _____

# Zoom Hog Bingo!

| | | | | |
|---|---|---|---|---|
| "Mentions their weekend plans." | "Says 'Just one more question.'" | "Suggests scheduling a follow-up meeting." | "Forgets to unmute before talking." | "Complains about technical difficulties." |
| "I know we're over time, but..." | Free | "Uses the word 'synergy' or 'circle back.'" | "Sorry, I didn't catch that—can you repeat it?" | "Thanks everyone at least three times." |
| "Let me just add one quick point." | "Talks about something unrelated to work." | "Asks for the slides or notes to be sent after the meeting." | "Repeats what someone else just said." | "Interrupts the speaker to make a point." |
| "Says 'Can everyone hear me?'" | "Joins late and asks to recap everything." | "Mentions their pet or child during the call." | "Asks a question unrelated to the topic." | "Talks over someone else." |
| "Goes on a long personal anecdote." | "Keeps their camera off and only chimes in to talk." | "Says 'I'll keep this brief' but doesn't." | "Can we circle back to what I said earlier?" | "Asks for clarification after it was explained." |

Name: _____

Date of meeting: _____

# Zoom Hog Bingo!

| | | | | |
|---|---|---|---|---|
| "Asks for input after everyone has already shared." | "Doesn't realize their camera is on." | "Argues over the meeting's purpose." | "Turns the camera off without explanation." | "Talks about their workout routine." |
| "Refers to an email no one has seen." | "Says 'I'll just follow up later.'" | Free | "Says 'This is off-topic, but...'" | "Blames their tech issues on the software." |
| "Asks for slides mid-meeting." | "Has kids running in the background." | "Complains about the meeting length." | "Asks to 'circle back to that later.'" | "Says 'Can we take a quick break?'" |
| "Says 'Can I play devil's advocate?'" | "Says 'Can we revisit this next week?'" | "Talks with their mouth full." | "Complains about meeting fatigue." | "Shares an unrequested opinion." |
| "Forgets to turn their mic off after the meeting ends." | "Gets frustrated about a tech issue." | "Interrupts the host to go back to their point." | "Describes their home office setup." | "Says 'Let's workshop this.'" |

Name: _____

Date of meeting: _____

# Zoom Hog Bingo!

| | | | | |
|---|---|---|---|---|
| "Says 'Let's put a pin in this.'" | "Explains the same point three different ways." | "Talks about their weekend in detail." | "Starts a sentence with 'In my experience...'" | "Asks to reschedule partway through." |
| "Says 'I'm not sure this is relevant, but...'" | "Laughs awkwardly after a bad joke." | "Says 'Just to piggyback on that...'" | "Asks for everyone's opinion on a minor issue." | "Rants about a minor issue." |
| "Gets frustrated about a tech issue." | "Leaves their mic on during private conversation." | "Requests the host to extend the meeting." | "Has their pet make a cameo on-screen." | "Mentions how much coffee they've had." |
| "Uses the phrase 'going forward.'" | "Uses jargon no one understands." | "Tells a story no one asked for." | "Requests to 'table this discussion.'" | "Keeps asking for more examples." |
| "Says 'Can you email me the notes?'" | Free | "Uses 'at the end of the day' excessively." | "Forgets they're muted when starting a long sentence." | "Complains about their kids being noisy." |

Name: _____

Date of meeting: _____

# Zoom Hog Bingo!

| | | | | |
|---|---|---|---|---|
| "Complains about the time of the meeting." | "Gives an overly detailed update." | "Says 'Can we take a step back for a second?'" | "Says 'Can you repeat that last part?'" | "Keeps calling the host by the wrong name." |
| "Says 'This is a silly question, but...'" | "Takes a phone call during the meeting." | "Asks 'Is everyone still here?'" | "Takes the discussion way off-topic." | "Forgets to share their screen properly." |
| "Suggests splitting into another meeting." | "Asks if everyone can see their screen." | "Asks for a topic to be discussed again." | "Uses a fun filter, like cat ears." | "Mutes and unmutes repeatedly." |
| "Clicks their pen loudly." | "Requests to stay longer after the meeting ends." | "Mentions the weather." | "Tries to explain technical issues in detail." | "Eats loudly during the call." |
| "Mentions their upcoming vacation." | "Talks about a personal problem." | "Loses their train of thought mid-sentence." | Free | "Says 'Let me circle back to that.'" |

Name: _____

Date of meeting: _____

# Zoom Hog Bingo!

| | | | | |
|---|---|---|---|---|
| "Asks if this meeting is being recorded." | "Says 'I'll email you later about this.'" | "Talks to someone off-screen during the call." | "Claims they didn't get the agenda." | "Repeats the same question multiple times." |
| "Talks about lunch plans." | "Mentions how tired they are." | "Complains about their camera not working." | "Explains something already covered." | "Joins from their car." |
| "Interrupts to say 'Let me rephrase that.'" | "Mentions their bad internet connection." | "Shares their screen without warning." | Free | "Uses a distracting virtual background." |
| "Uses 'umm' excessively." | "Says 'This will only take a minute.'" | "Mentions how busy they are." | "Starts with 'This might be a stupid question, but...'" | "Talks over the host." |
| "Has loud background noise." | "Cracks an awkward joke that no one laughs at." | "Turns off their camera mid-meeting." | "Asks for a poll to be done." | "Overexplains their point." |

Name: _____

Date of meeting: _____

# Zoom Hog Bingo!

| | | | | |
|---|---|---|---|---|
| "Mentions their weekend plans." | "Says 'Just one more question.'" | "Suggests scheduling a follow-up meeting." | "Forgets to unmute before talking." | "Complains about technical difficulties." |
| "I know we're over time, but..." | Free | "Uses the word 'synergy' or 'circle back.'" | "Sorry, I didn't catch that—can you repeat it?" | "Thanks everyone at least three times." |
| "Let me just add one quick point." | "Talks about something unrelated to work." | "Asks for the slides or notes to be sent after the meeting." | "Repeats what someone else just said." | "Interrupts the speaker to make a point." |
| "Says 'Can everyone hear me?'" | "Joins late and asks to recap everything." | "Mentions their pet or child during the call." | "Asks a question unrelated to the topic." | "Talks over someone else." |
| "Goes on a long personal anecdote." | "Keeps their camera off and only chimes in to talk." | "Says 'I'll keep this brief' but doesn't." | "Can we circle back to what I said earlier?" | "Asks for clarification after it was explained." |

Name: _____

Date of meeting: _____

# Zoom Hog Bingo!

| | | | | |
|---|---|---|---|---|
| "Asks for input after everyone has already shared." | "Doesn't realize their camera is on." | "Argues over the meeting's purpose." | "Turns the camera off without explanation." | "Talks about their workout routine." |
| "Refers to an email no one has seen." | "Says 'I'll just follow up later.'" | Free | "Says 'This is off-topic, but...'" | "Blames their tech issues on the software." |
| "Asks for slides mid-meeting." | "Has kids running in the background." | "Complains about the meeting length." | "Asks to 'circle back to that later.'" | "Says 'Can we take a quick break?'" |
| "Says 'Can I play devil's advocate?'" | "Says 'Can we revisit this next week?'" | "Talks with their mouth full." | "Complains about meeting fatigue." | "Shares an unrequested opinion." |
| "Forgets to turn their mic off after the meeting ends." | "Gets frustrated about a tech issue." | "Interrupts the host to go back to their point." | "Describes their home office setup." | "Says 'Let's workshop this.'" |

Name: _____

Date of meeting: _____

# Zoom Hog Bingo!

| | | | | |
|---|---|---|---|---|
| "Says 'Let's put a pin in this.'" | "Explains the same point three different ways." | "Talks about their weekend in detail." | "Starts a sentence with 'In my experience...'" | "Asks to reschedule partway through." |
| "Says 'I'm not sure this is relevant, but...'" | "Laughs awkwardly after a bad joke." | "Says 'Just to piggyback on that...'" | "Asks for everyone's opinion on a minor issue." | "Rants about a minor issue." |
| "Gets frustrated about a tech issue." | "Leaves their mic on during private conversation." | "Requests the host to extend the meeting." | "Has their pet make a cameo on-screen." | "Mentions how much coffee they've had." |
| "Uses the phrase 'going forward.'" | "Uses jargon no one understands." | "Tells a story no one asked for." | "Requests to 'table this discussion.'" | "Keeps asking for more examples." |
| "Says 'Can you email me the notes?'" | Free | "Uses 'at the end of the day' excessively." | "Forgets they're muted when starting a long sentence." | "Complains about their kids being noisy." |

Name: _____

Date of meeting: _____

# Zoom Hog Bingo!

| | | | | |
|---|---|---|---|---|
| "Complains about the time of the meeting." | "Gives an overly detailed update." | "Says 'Can we take a step back for a second?'" | "Says 'Can you repeat that last part?'" | "Keeps calling the host by the wrong name." |
| "Says 'This is a silly question, but...'" | "Takes a phone call during the meeting." | "Asks 'Is everyone still here?'" | "Takes the discussion way off-topic." | "Forgets to share their screen properly." |
| "Suggests splitting into another meeting." | "Asks if everyone can see their screen." | "Asks for a topic to be discussed again." | "Uses a fun filter, like cat ears." | "Mutes and unmutes repeatedly." |
| "Clicks their pen loudly." | "Requests to stay longer after the meeting ends." | "Mentions the weather." | "Tries to explain technical issues in detail." | "Eats loudly during the call." |
| "Mentions their upcoming vacation." | "Talks about a personal problem." | "Loses their train of thought mid-sentence." | Free | "Says 'Let me circle back to that.'" |

Name: _____

Date of meeting: _____

# Zoom Hog Bingo!

| | | | | |
|---|---|---|---|---|
| "Asks if this meeting is being recorded." | "Says 'I'll email you later about this.'" | "Talks to someone off-screen during the call." | "Claims they didn't get the agenda." | "Repeats the same question multiple times." |
| "Talks about lunch plans." | "Mentions how tired they are." | "Complains about their camera not working." | "Explains something already covered." | "Joins from their car." |
| "Interrupts to say 'Let me rephrase that.'" | "Mentions their bad internet connection." | "Shares their screen without warning." | Free | "Uses a distracting virtual background." |
| "Uses 'umm' excessively." | "Says 'This will only take a minute.'" | "Mentions how busy they are." | "Starts with 'This might be a stupid question, but...'" | "Talks over the host." |
| "Has loud background noise." | "Cracks an awkward joke that no one laughs at." | "Turns off their camera mid-meeting." | "Asks for a poll to be done." | "Overexplains their point." |

Name: _____

Date of meeting: _____

# Zoom Hog Bingo!

| | | | | |
|---|---|---|---|---|
| "Mentions their weekend plans." | "Says 'Just one more question.'" | "Suggests scheduling a follow-up meeting." | "Forgets to unmute before talking." | "Complains about technical difficulties." |
| "I know we're over time, but..." | Free | "Uses the word 'synergy' or 'circle back.'" | "Sorry, I didn't catch that—can you repeat it?" | "Thanks everyone at least three times." |
| "Let me just add one quick point." | "Talks about something unrelated to work." | "Asks for the slides or notes to be sent after the meeting." | "Repeats what someone else just said." | "Interrupts the speaker to make a point." |
| "Says 'Can everyone hear me?'" | "Joins late and asks to recap everything." | "Mentions their pet or child during the call." | "Asks a question unrelated to the topic." | "Talks over someone else." |
| "Goes on a long personal anecdote." | "Keeps their camera off and only chimes in to talk." | "Says 'I'll keep this brief' but doesn't." | "Can we circle back to what I said earlier?" | "Asks for clarification after it was explained." |

Name: _____

Date of meeting: _____

# Zoom Hog Bingo!

| | | | | |
|---|---|---|---|---|
| "Asks for input after everyone has already shared." | "Doesn't realize their camera is on." | "Argues over the meeting's purpose." | "Turns the camera off without explanation." | "Talks about their workout routine." |
| "Refers to an email no one has seen." | "Says 'I'll just follow up later.'" | Free | "Says 'This is off-topic, but...'" | "Blames their tech issues on the software." |
| "Asks for slides mid-meeting." | "Has kids running in the background." | "Complains about the meeting length." | "Asks to 'circle back to that later.'" | "Says 'Can we take a quick break?'" |
| "Says 'Can I play devil's advocate?'" | "Says 'Can we revisit this next week?'" | "Talks with their mouth full." | "Complains about meeting fatigue." | "Shares an unrequested opinion." |
| "Forgets to turn their mic off after the meeting ends." | "Gets frustrated about a tech issue." | "Interrupts the host to go back to their point." | "Describes their home office setup." | "Says 'Let's workshop this.'" |

Name: _____

Date of meeting: _____

# Zoom Hog Bingo!

| | | | | |
|---|---|---|---|---|
| "Says 'Let's put a pin in this.'" | "Explains the same point three different ways." | "Talks about their weekend in detail." | "Starts a sentence with 'In my experience...'" | "Asks to reschedule partway through." |
| "Says 'I'm not sure this is relevant, but...'" | "Laughs awkwardly after a bad joke." | "Says 'Just to piggyback on that...'" | "Asks for everyone's opinion on a minor issue." | "Rants about a minor issue." |
| "Gets frustrated about a tech issue." | "Leaves their mic on during private conversation." | "Requests the host to extend the meeting." | "Has their pet make a cameo on-screen." | "Mentions how much coffee they've had." |
| "Uses the phrase 'going forward.'" | "Uses jargon no one understands." | "Tells a story no one asked for." | "Requests to 'table this discussion.'" | "Keeps asking for more examples." |
| "Says 'Can you email me the notes?'" | Free | "Uses 'at the end of the day' excessively." | "Forgets they're muted when starting a long sentence." | "Complains about their kids being noisy." |

Name: _____

Date of meeting: _____

# Zoom Hog Bingo!

| | | | | |
|---|---|---|---|---|
| "Complains about the time of the meeting." | "Gives an overly detailed update." | "Says 'Can we take a step back for a second?'" | "Says 'Can you repeat that last part?'" | "Keeps calling the host by the wrong name." |
| "Says 'This is a silly question, but...'" | "Takes a phone call during the meeting." | "Asks 'Is everyone still here?'" | "Takes the discussion way off-topic." | "Forgets to share their screen properly." |
| "Suggests splitting into another meeting." | "Asks if everyone can see their screen." | "Asks for a topic to be discussed again." | "Uses a fun filter, like cat ears." | "Mutes and unmutes repeatedly." |
| "Clicks their pen loudly." | "Requests to stay longer after the meeting ends." | "Mentions the weather." | "Tries to explain technical issues in detail." | "Eats loudly during the call." |
| "Mentions their upcoming vacation." | "Talks about a personal problem." | "Loses their train of thought mid-sentence." | Free | "Says 'Let me circle back to that.'" |

Name: _____

Date of meeting: _____

# Zoom Hog Bingo!

| | | | | |
|---|---|---|---|---|
| "Asks if this meeting is being recorded." | "Says 'I'll email you later about this.'" | "Talks to someone off-screen during the call." | "Claims they didn't get the agenda." | "Repeats the same question multiple times." |
| "Talks about lunch plans." | "Mentions how tired they are." | "Complains about their camera not working." | "Explains something already covered." | "Joins from their car." |
| "Interrupts to say 'Let me rephrase that.'" | "Mentions their bad internet connection." | "Shares their screen without warning." | Free | "Uses a distracting virtual background." |
| "Uses 'umm' excessively." | "Says 'This will only take a minute.'" | "Mentions how busy they are." | "Starts with 'This might be a stupid question, but...'" | "Talks over the host." |
| "Has loud background noise." | "Cracks an awkward joke that no one laughs at." | "Turns off their camera mid-meeting." | "Asks for a poll to be done." | "Overexplains their point." |

Name: _____

Date of meeting: _____

# Zoom Hog Bingo!

| | | | | |
|---|---|---|---|---|
| "Mentions their weekend plans." | "Says 'Just one more question.'" | "Suggests scheduling a follow-up meeting." | "Forgets to unmute before talking." | "Complains about technical difficulties." |
| "I know we're over time, but..." | Free | "Uses the word 'synergy' or 'circle back.'" | "Sorry, I didn't catch that—can you repeat it?" | "Thanks everyone at least three times." |
| "Let me just add one quick point." | "Talks about something unrelated to work." | "Asks for the slides or notes to be sent after the meeting." | "Repeats what someone else just said." | "Interrupts the speaker to make a point." |
| "Says 'Can everyone hear me?'" | "Joins late and asks to recap everything." | "Mentions their pet or child during the call." | "Asks a question unrelated to the topic." | "Talks over someone else." |
| "Goes on a long personal anecdote." | "Keeps their camera off and only chimes in to talk." | "Says 'I'll keep this brief' but doesn't." | "Can we circle back to what I said earlier?" | "Asks for clarification after it was explained." |

Name: _____

Date of meeting: _____

# Zoom Hog Bingo!

| | | | | |
|---|---|---|---|---|
| "Asks for input after everyone has already shared." | "Doesn't realize their camera is on." | "Argues over the meeting's purpose." | "Turns the camera off without explanation." | "Talks about their workout routine." |
| "Refers to an email no one has seen." | "Says 'I'll just follow up later.'" | Free | "Says 'This is off-topic, but...'" | "Blames their tech issues on the software." |
| "Asks for slides mid-meeting." | "Has kids running in the background." | "Complains about the meeting length." | "Asks to 'circle back to that later.'" | "Says 'Can we take a quick break?'" |
| "Says 'Can I play devil's advocate?'" | "Says 'Can we revisit this next week?'" | "Talks with their mouth full." | "Complains about meeting fatigue." | "Shares an unrequested opinion." |
| "Forgets to turn their mic off after the meeting ends." | "Gets frustrated about a tech issue." | "Interrupts the host to go back to their point." | "Describes their home office setup." | "Says 'Let's workshop this.'" |

Name: _____

Date of meeting: _____

# Zoom Hog Bingo!

| | | | | |
|---|---|---|---|---|
| "Says 'Let's put a pin in this.'" | "Explains the same point three different ways." | "Talks about their weekend in detail." | "Starts a sentence with 'In my experience...'" | "Asks to reschedule partway through." |
| "Says 'I'm not sure this is relevant, but...'" | "Laughs awkwardly after a bad joke." | "Says 'Just to piggyback on that...'" | "Asks for everyone's opinion on a minor issue." | "Rants about a minor issue." |
| "Gets frustrated about a tech issue." | "Leaves their mic on during private conversation." | "Requests the host to extend the meeting." | "Has their pet make a cameo on-screen." | "Mentions how much coffee they've had." |
| "Uses the phrase 'going forward.'" | "Uses jargon no one understands." | "Tells a story no one asked for." | "Requests to 'table this discussion.'" | "Keeps asking for more examples." |
| "Says 'Can you email me the notes?'" | Free | "Uses 'at the end of the day' excessively." | "Forgets they're muted when starting a long sentence." | "Complains about their kids being noisy." |

Name: _____

Date of meeting: _____

# Zoom Hog Bingo!

| | | | | |
|---|---|---|---|---|
| "Complains about the time of the meeting." | "Gives an overly detailed update." | "Says 'Can we take a step back for a second?'" | "Says 'Can you repeat that last part?'" | "Keeps calling the host by the wrong name." |
| "Says 'This is a silly question, but...'" | "Takes a phone call during the meeting." | "Asks 'Is everyone still here?'" | "Takes the discussion way off-topic." | "Forgets to share their screen properly." |
| "Suggests splitting into another meeting." | "Asks if everyone can see their screen." | "Asks for a topic to be discussed again." | "Uses a fun filter, like cat ears." | "Mutes and unmutes repeatedly." |
| "Clicks their pen loudly." | "Requests to stay longer after the meeting ends." | "Mentions the weather." | "Tries to explain technical issues in detail." | "Eats loudly during the call." |
| "Mentions their upcoming vacation." | "Talks about a personal problem." | "Loses their train of thought mid-sentence." | Free | "Says 'Let me circle back to that.'" |

Name: _____

Date of meeting: _____

# Zoom Hog Bingo!

| | | | | |
|---|---|---|---|---|
| "Asks if this meeting is being recorded." | "Says 'I'll email you later about this.'" | "Talks to someone off-screen during the call." | "Claims they didn't get the agenda." | "Repeats the same question multiple times." |
| "Talks about lunch plans." | "Mentions how tired they are." | "Complains about their camera not working." | "Explains something already covered." | "Joins from their car." |
| "Interrupts to say 'Let me rephrase that.'" | "Mentions their bad internet connection." | "Shares their screen without warning." | Free | "Uses a distracting virtual background." |
| "Uses 'umm' excessively." | "Says 'This will only take a minute.'" | "Mentions how busy they are." | "Starts with 'This might be a stupid question, but...'" | "Talks over the host." |
| "Has loud background noise." | "Cracks an awkward joke that no one laughs at." | "Turns off their camera mid-meeting." | "Asks for a poll to be done." | "Overexplains their point." |

Name: _____

Date of meeting: _____

# Zoom Hog Bingo!

| | | | | |
|---|---|---|---|---|
| "Mentions their weekend plans." | "Says 'Just one more question.'" | "Suggests scheduling a follow-up meeting." | "Forgets to unmute before talking." | "Complains about technical difficulties." |
| "I know we're over time, but…" | Free | "Uses the word 'synergy' or 'circle back.'" | "Sorry, I didn't catch that—can you repeat it?" | "Thanks everyone at least three times." |
| "Let me just add one quick point." | "Talks about something unrelated to work." | "Asks for the slides or notes to be sent after the meeting." | "Repeats what someone else just said." | "Interrupts the speaker to make a point." |
| "Says 'Can everyone hear me?'" | "Joins late and asks to recap everything." | "Mentions their pet or child during the call." | "Asks a question unrelated to the topic." | "Talks over someone else." |
| "Goes on a long personal anecdote." | "Keeps their camera off and only chimes in to talk." | "Says 'I'll keep this brief' but doesn't." | "Can we circle back to what I said earlier?" | "Asks for clarification after it was explained." |

Name: _____

Date of meeting: _____

# Zoom Hog Bingo!

| | | | | |
|---|---|---|---|---|
| "Asks for input after everyone has already shared." | "Doesn't realize their camera is on." | "Argues over the meeting's purpose." | "Turns the camera off without explanation." | "Talks about their workout routine." |
| "Refers to an email no one has seen." | "Says 'I'll just follow up later.'" | Free | "Says 'This is off-topic, but...'" | "Blames their tech issues on the software." |
| "Asks for slides mid-meeting." | "Has kids running in the background." | "Complains about the meeting length." | "Asks to 'circle back to that later.'" | "Says 'Can we take a quick break?'" |
| "Says 'Can I play devil's advocate?'" | "Says 'Can we revisit this next week?'" | "Talks with their mouth full." | "Complains about meeting fatigue." | "Shares an unrequested opinion." |
| "Forgets to turn their mic off after the meeting ends." | "Gets frustrated about a tech issue." | "Interrupts the host to go back to their point." | "Describes their home office setup." | "Says 'Let's workshop this.'" |

Name: _____

Date of meeting: _____

# Zoom Hog Bingo!

| | | | | |
|---|---|---|---|---|
| "Says 'Let's put a pin in this.'" | "Explains the same point three different ways." | "Talks about their weekend in detail." | "Starts a sentence with 'In my experience...'" | "Asks to reschedule partway through." |
| "Says 'I'm not sure this is relevant, but...'" | "Laughs awkwardly after a bad joke." | "Says 'Just to piggyback on that...'" | "Asks for everyone's opinion on a minor issue." | "Rants about a minor issue." |
| "Gets frustrated about a tech issue." | "Leaves their mic on during private conversation." | "Requests the host to extend the meeting." | "Has their pet make a cameo on-screen." | "Mentions how much coffee they've had." |
| "Uses the phrase 'going forward.'" | "Uses jargon no one understands." | "Tells a story no one asked for." | "Requests to 'table this discussion.'" | "Keeps asking for more examples." |
| "Says 'Can you email me the notes?'" | Free | "Uses 'at the end of the day' excessively." | "Forgets they're muted when starting a long sentence." | "Complains about their kids being noisy." |

Name: _____

Date of meeting: _____

# Zoom Hog Bingo!

| | | | | |
|---|---|---|---|---|
| "Complains about the time of the meeting." | "Gives an overly detailed update." | "Says 'Can we take a step back for a second?'" | "Says 'Can you repeat that last part?'" | "Keeps calling the host by the wrong name." |
| "Says 'This is a silly question, but...'" | "Takes a phone call during the meeting." | "Asks 'Is everyone still here?'" | "Takes the discussion way off-topic." | "Forgets to share their screen properly." |
| "Suggests splitting into another meeting." | "Asks if everyone can see their screen." | "Asks for a topic to be discussed again." | "Uses a fun filter, like cat ears." | "Mutes and unmutes repeatedly." |
| "Clicks their pen loudly." | "Requests to stay longer after the meeting ends." | "Mentions the weather." | "Tries to explain technical issues in detail." | "Eats loudly during the call." |
| "Mentions their upcoming vacation." | "Talks about a personal problem." | "Loses their train of thought mid-sentence." | Free | "Says 'Let me circle back to that.'" |

Name: _____

Date of meeting: _____

# Zoom Hog Bingo!

| | | | | |
|---|---|---|---|---|
| "Asks if this meeting is being recorded." | "Says 'I'll email you later about this.'" | "Talks to someone off-screen during the call." | "Claims they didn't get the agenda." | "Repeats the same question multiple times." |
| "Talks about lunch plans." | "Mentions how tired they are." | "Complains about their camera not working." | "Explains something already covered." | "Joins from their car." |
| "Interrupts to say 'Let me rephrase that.'" | "Mentions their bad internet connection." | "Shares their screen without warning." | Free | "Uses a distracting virtual background." |
| "Uses 'umm' excessively." | "Says 'This will only take a minute.'" | "Mentions how busy they are." | "Starts with 'This might be a stupid question, but...'" | "Talks over the host." |
| "Has loud background noise." | "Cracks an awkward joke that no one laughs at." | "Turns off their camera mid-meeting." | "Asks for a poll to be done." | "Overexplains their point." |

Name: _____

Date of meeting: _____

# Zoom Hog Bingo!

| | | | | |
|---|---|---|---|---|
| "Mentions their weekend plans." | "Says 'Just one more question.'" | "Suggests scheduling a follow-up meeting." | "Forgets to unmute before talking." | "Complains about technical difficulties." |
| "I know we're over time, but..." | Free | "Uses the word 'synergy' or 'circle back.'" | "Sorry, I didn't catch that—can you repeat it?" | "Thanks everyone at least three times." |
| "Let me just add one quick point." | "Talks about something unrelated to work." | "Asks for the slides or notes to be sent after the meeting." | "Repeats what someone else just said." | "Interrupts the speaker to make a point." |
| "Says 'Can everyone hear me?'" | "Joins late and asks to recap everything." | "Mentions their pet or child during the call." | "Asks a question unrelated to the topic." | "Talks over someone else." |
| "Goes on a long personal anecdote." | "Keeps their camera off and only chimes in to talk." | "Says 'I'll keep this brief' but doesn't." | "Can we circle back to what I said earlier?" | "Asks for clarification after it was explained." |

Name: _____

Date of meeting: _____

# Zoom Hog Bingo!

| | | | | |
|---|---|---|---|---|
| "Asks for input after everyone has already shared." | "Doesn't realize their camera is on." | "Argues over the meeting's purpose." | "Turns the camera off without explanation." | "Talks about their workout routine." |
| "Refers to an email no one has seen." | "Says 'I'll just follow up later.'" | Free | "Says 'This is off-topic, but...'" | "Blames their tech issues on the software." |
| "Asks for slides mid-meeting." | "Has kids running in the background." | "Complains about the meeting length." | "Asks to 'circle back to that later.'" | "Says 'Can we take a quick break?'" |
| "Says 'Can I play devil's advocate?'" | "Says 'Can we revisit this next week?'" | "Talks with their mouth full." | "Complains about meeting fatigue." | "Shares an unrequested opinion." |
| "Forgets to turn their mic off after the meeting ends." | "Gets frustrated about a tech issue." | "Interrupts the host to go back to their point." | "Describes their home office setup." | "Says 'Let's workshop this.'" |

Name: _____

Date of meeting: _____

# Zoom Hog Bingo!

| | | | | |
|---|---|---|---|---|
| "Says 'Let's put a pin in this.'" | "Explains the same point three different ways." | "Talks about their weekend in detail." | "Starts a sentence with 'In my experience...'" | "Asks to reschedule partway through." |
| "Says 'I'm not sure this is relevant, but...'" | "Laughs awkwardly after a bad joke." | "Says 'Just to piggyback on that...'" | "Asks for everyone's opinion on a minor issue." | "Rants about a minor issue." |
| "Gets frustrated about a tech issue." | "Leaves their mic on during private conversation." | "Requests the host to extend the meeting." | "Has their pet make a cameo on-screen." | "Mentions how much coffee they've had." |
| "Uses the phrase 'going forward.'" | "Uses jargon no one understands." | "Tells a story no one asked for." | "Requests to 'table this discussion.'" | "Keeps asking for more examples." |
| "Says 'Can you email me the notes?'" | Free | "Uses 'at the end of the day' excessively." | "Forgets they're muted when starting a long sentence." | "Complains about their kids being noisy." |

Name: _____

Date of meeting: _____

# Zoom Hog Bingo!

| | | | | |
|---|---|---|---|---|
| "Complains about the time of the meeting." | "Gives an overly detailed update." | "Says 'Can we take a step back for a second?'" | "Says 'Can you repeat that last part?'" | "Keeps calling the host by the wrong name." |
| "Says 'This is a silly question, but...'" | "Takes a phone call during the meeting." | "Asks 'Is everyone still here?'" | "Takes the discussion way off-topic." | "Forgets to share their screen properly." |
| "Suggests splitting into another meeting." | "Asks if everyone can see their screen." | "Asks for a topic to be discussed again." | "Uses a fun filter, like cat ears." | "Mutes and unmutes repeatedly." |
| "Clicks their pen loudly." | "Requests to stay longer after the meeting ends." | "Mentions the weather." | "Tries to explain technical issues in detail." | "Eats loudly during the call." |
| "Mentions their upcoming vacation." | "Talks about a personal problem." | "Loses their train of thought mid-sentence." | Free | "Says 'Let me circle back to that.'" |

Name: _____

Date of meeting: _____

# Zoom Hog Bingo!

| | | | | |
|---|---|---|---|---|
| "Asks if this meeting is being recorded." | "Says 'I'll email you later about this.'" | "Talks to someone off-screen during the call." | "Claims they didn't get the agenda." | "Repeats the same question multiple times." |
| "Talks about lunch plans." | "Mentions how tired they are." | "Complains about their camera not working." | "Explains something already covered." | "Joins from their car." |
| "Interrupts to say 'Let me rephrase that.'" | "Mentions their bad internet connection." | "Shares their screen without warning." | Free | "Uses a distracting virtual background." |
| "Uses 'umm' excessively." | "Says 'This will only take a minute.'" | "Mentions how busy they are." | "Starts with 'This might be a stupid question, but...'" | "Talks over the host." |
| "Has loud background noise." | "Cracks an awkward joke that no one laughs at." | "Turns off their camera mid-meeting." | "Asks for a poll to be done." | "Overexplains their point." |

Name: _____

Date of meeting: _____

# Zoom Hog Bingo!

| | | | | |
|---|---|---|---|---|
| "Mentions their weekend plans." | "Says 'Just one more question.'" | "Suggests scheduling a follow-up meeting." | "Forgets to unmute before talking." | "Complains about technical difficulties." |
| "I know we're over time, but..." | Free | "Uses the word 'synergy' or 'circle back.'" | "Sorry, I didn't catch that—can you repeat it?" | "Thanks everyone at least three times." |
| "Let me just add one quick point." | "Talks about something unrelated to work." | "Asks for the slides or notes to be sent after the meeting." | "Repeats what someone else just said." | "Interrupts the speaker to make a point." |
| "Says 'Can everyone hear me?'" | "Joins late and asks to recap everything." | "Mentions their pet or child during the call." | "Asks a question unrelated to the topic." | "Talks over someone else." |
| "Goes on a long personal anecdote." | "Keeps their camera off and only chimes in to talk." | "Says 'I'll keep this brief' but doesn't." | "Can we circle back to what I said earlier?" | "Asks for clarification after it was explained." |

Name: _____

Date of meeting: _____

# Zoom Hog Bingo!

| | | | | |
|---|---|---|---|---|
| "Asks for input after everyone has already shared." | "Doesn't realize their camera is on." | "Argues over the meeting's purpose." | "Turns the camera off without explanation." | "Talks about their workout routine." |
| "Refers to an email no one has seen." | "Says 'I'll just follow up later.'" | Free | "Says 'This is off-topic, but...'" | "Blames their tech issues on the software." |
| "Asks for slides mid-meeting." | "Has kids running in the background." | "Complains about the meeting length." | "Asks to 'circle back to that later.'" | "Says 'Can we take a quick break?'" |
| "Says 'Can I play devil's advocate?'" | "Says 'Can we revisit this next week?'" | "Talks with their mouth full." | "Complains about meeting fatigue." | "Shares an unrequested opinion." |
| "Forgets to turn their mic off after the meeting ends." | "Gets frustrated about a tech issue." | "Interrupts the host to go back to their point." | "Describes their home office setup." | "Says 'Let's workshop this.'" |

Name: _____

Date of meeting: _____

# Zoom Hog Bingo!

| | | | | |
|---|---|---|---|---|
| "Says 'Let's put a pin in this.'" | "Explains the same point three different ways." | "Talks about their weekend in detail." | "Starts a sentence with 'In my experience...'" | "Asks to reschedule partway through." |
| "Says 'I'm not sure this is relevant, but...'" | "Laughs awkwardly after a bad joke." | "Says 'Just to piggyback on that...'" | "Asks for everyone's opinion on a minor issue." | "Rants about a minor issue." |
| "Gets frustrated about a tech issue." | "Leaves their mic on during private conversation." | "Requests the host to extend the meeting." | "Has their pet make a cameo on-screen." | "Mentions how much coffee they've had." |
| "Uses the phrase 'going forward.'" | "Uses jargon no one understands." | "Tells a story no one asked for." | "Requests to 'table this discussion.'" | "Keeps asking for more examples." |
| "Says 'Can you email me the notes?'" | Free | "Uses 'at the end of the day' excessively." | "Forgets they're muted when starting a long sentence." | "Complains about their kids being noisy." |

Name: _____

Date of meeting: _____

# Zoom Hog Bingo!

| | | | | |
|---|---|---|---|---|
| "Complains about the time of the meeting." | "Gives an overly detailed update." | "Says 'Can we take a step back for a second?'" | "Says 'Can you repeat that last part?'" | "Keeps calling the host by the wrong name." |
| "Says 'This is a silly question, but...'" | "Takes a phone call during the meeting." | "Asks 'Is everyone still here?'" | "Takes the discussion way off-topic." | "Forgets to share their screen properly." |
| "Suggests splitting into another meeting." | "Asks if everyone can see their screen." | "Asks for a topic to be discussed again." | "Uses a fun filter, like cat ears." | "Mutes and unmutes repeatedly." |
| "Clicks their pen loudly." | "Requests to stay longer after the meeting ends." | "Mentions the weather." | "Tries to explain technical issues in detail." | "Eats loudly during the call." |
| "Mentions their upcoming vacation." | "Talks about a personal problem." | "Loses their train of thought mid-sentence." | Free | "Says 'Let me circle back to that.'" |

Name: _____

Date of meeting: _____

# Zoom Hog Bingo!

| | | | | |
|---|---|---|---|---|
| "Asks if this meeting is being recorded." | "Says 'I'll email you later about this.'" | "Talks to someone off-screen during the call." | "Claims they didn't get the agenda." | "Repeats the same question multiple times." |
| "Talks about lunch plans." | "Mentions how tired they are." | "Complains about their camera not working." | "Explains something already covered." | "Joins from their car." |
| "Interrupts to say 'Let me rephrase that.'" | "Mentions their bad internet connection." | "Shares their screen without warning." | Free | "Uses a distracting virtual background." |
| "Uses 'umm' excessively." | "Says 'This will only take a minute.'" | "Mentions how busy they are." | "Starts with 'This might be a stupid question, but...'" | "Talks over the host." |
| "Has loud background noise." | "Cracks an awkward joke that no one laughs at." | "Turns off their camera mid-meeting." | "Asks for a poll to be done." | "Overexplains their point." |

Name: _____

Date of meeting: _____

# Zoom Hog Bingo!

| "Mentions their weekend plans." | "Says 'Just one more question.'" | "Suggests scheduling a follow-up meeting." | "Forgets to unmute before talking." | "Complains about technical difficulties." |
|---|---|---|---|---|
| "I know we're over time, but..." | Free | "Uses the word 'synergy' or 'circle back.'" | "Sorry, I didn't catch that—can you repeat it?" | "Thanks everyone at least three times." |
| "Let me just add one quick point." | "Talks about something unrelated to work." | "Asks for the slides or notes to be sent after the meeting." | "Repeats what someone else just said." | "Interrupts the speaker to make a point." |
| "Says 'Can everyone hear me?'" | "Joins late and asks to recap everything." | "Mentions their pet or child during the call." | "Asks a question unrelated to the topic." | "Talks over someone else." |
| "Goes on a long personal anecdote." | "Keeps their camera off and only chimes in to talk." | "Says 'I'll keep this brief' but doesn't." | "Can we circle back to what I said earlier?" | "Asks for clarification after it was explained." |

Name: _____

Date of meeting: _____

# Zoom Hog Bingo!

| | | | | |
|---|---|---|---|---|
| "Asks for input after everyone has already shared." | "Doesn't realize their camera is on." | "Argues over the meeting's purpose." | "Turns the camera off without explanation." | "Talks about their workout routine." |
| "Refers to an email no one has seen." | "Says 'I'll just follow up later.'" | Free | "Says 'This is off-topic, but...'" | "Blames their tech issues on the software." |
| "Asks for slides mid-meeting." | "Has kids running in the background." | "Complains about the meeting length." | "Asks to 'circle back to that later.'" | "Says 'Can we take a quick break?'" |
| "Says 'Can I play devil's advocate?'" | "Says 'Can we revisit this next week?'" | "Talks with their mouth full." | "Complains about meeting fatigue." | "Shares an unrequested opinion." |
| "Forgets to turn their mic off after the meeting ends." | "Gets frustrated about a tech issue." | "Interrupts the host to go back to their point." | "Describes their home office setup." | "Says 'Let's workshop this.'" |

Name: _____

Date of meeting: _____

# Zoom Hog Bingo!

| | | | | |
|---|---|---|---|---|
| "Says 'Let's put a pin in this.'" | "Explains the same point three different ways." | "Talks about their weekend in detail." | "Starts a sentence with 'In my experience...'" | "Asks to reschedule partway through." |
| "Says 'I'm not sure this is relevant, but...'" | "Laughs awkwardly after a bad joke." | "Says 'Just to piggyback on that...'" | "Asks for everyone's opinion on a minor issue." | "Rants about a minor issue." |
| "Gets frustrated about a tech issue." | "Leaves their mic on during private conversation." | "Requests the host to extend the meeting." | "Has their pet make a cameo on-screen." | "Mentions how much coffee they've had." |
| "Uses the phrase 'going forward.'" | "Uses jargon no one understands." | "Tells a story no one asked for." | "Requests to 'table this discussion.'" | "Keeps asking for more examples." |
| "Says 'Can you email me the notes?'" | Free | "Uses 'at the end of the day' excessively." | "Forgets they're muted when starting a long sentence." | "Complains about their kids being noisy." |

Name: _____

Date of meeting: _____

# Zoom Hog Bingo!

| | | | | |
|---|---|---|---|---|
| "Complains about the time of the meeting." | "Gives an overly detailed update." | "Says 'Can we take a step back for a second?'" | "Says 'Can you repeat that last part?'" | "Keeps calling the host by the wrong name." |
| "Says 'This is a silly question, but...'" | "Takes a phone call during the meeting." | "Asks 'Is everyone still here?'" | "Takes the discussion way off-topic." | "Forgets to share their screen properly." |
| "Suggests splitting into another meeting." | "Asks if everyone can see their screen." | "Asks for a topic to be discussed again." | "Uses a fun filter, like cat ears." | "Mutes and unmutes repeatedly." |
| "Clicks their pen loudly." | "Requests to stay longer after the meeting ends." | "Mentions the weather." | "Tries to explain technical issues in detail." | "Eats loudly during the call." |
| "Mentions their upcoming vacation." | "Talks about a personal problem." | "Loses their train of thought mid-sentence." | Free | "Says 'Let me circle back to that.'" |

Name: _____

Date of meeting: _____

# Zoom Hog Bingo!

| | | | | |
|---|---|---|---|---|
| "Asks if this meeting is being recorded." | "Says 'I'll email you later about this.'" | "Talks to someone off-screen during the call." | "Claims they didn't get the agenda." | "Repeats the same question multiple times." |
| "Talks about lunch plans." | "Mentions how tired they are." | "Complains about their camera not working." | "Explains something already covered." | "Joins from their car." |
| "Interrupts to say 'Let me rephrase that.'" | "Mentions their bad internet connection." | "Shares their screen without warning." | Free | "Uses a distracting virtual background." |
| "Uses 'umm' excessively." | "Says 'This will only take a minute.'" | "Mentions how busy they are." | "Starts with 'This might be a stupid question, but...'" | "Talks over the host." |
| "Has loud background noise." | "Cracks an awkward joke that no one laughs at." | "Turns off their camera mid-meeting." | "Asks for a poll to be done." | "Overexplains their point." |

Name: _____

Date of meeting: _____

# Zoom Hog Bingo!

| | | | | |
|---|---|---|---|---|
| "Mentions their weekend plans." | "Says 'Just one more question.'" | "Suggests scheduling a follow-up meeting." | "Forgets to unmute before talking." | "Complains about technical difficulties." |
| "I know we're over time, but..." | Free | "Uses the word 'synergy' or 'circle back.'" | "Sorry, I didn't catch that—can you repeat it?" | "Thanks everyone at least three times." |
| "Let me just add one quick point." | "Talks about something unrelated to work." | "Asks for the slides or notes to be sent after the meeting." | "Repeats what someone else just said." | "Interrupts the speaker to make a point." |
| "Says 'Can everyone hear me?'" | "Joins late and asks to recap everything." | "Mentions their pet or child during the call." | "Asks a question unrelated to the topic." | "Talks over someone else." |
| "Goes on a long personal anecdote." | "Keeps their camera off and only chimes in to talk." | "Says 'I'll keep this brief' but doesn't." | "Can we circle back to what I said earlier?" | "Asks for clarification after it was explained." |

Name: _____

Date of meeting: _____

# Zoom Hog Bingo!

| | | | | |
|---|---|---|---|---|
| "Asks for input after everyone has already shared." | "Doesn't realize their camera is on." | "Argues over the meeting's purpose." | "Turns the camera off without explanation." | "Talks about their workout routine." |
| "Refers to an email no one has seen." | "Says 'I'll just follow up later.'" | Free | "Says 'This is off-topic, but...'" | "Blames their tech issues on the software." |
| "Asks for slides mid-meeting." | "Has kids running in the background." | "Complains about the meeting length." | "Asks to 'circle back to that later.'" | "Says 'Can we take a quick break?'" |
| "Says 'Can I play devil's advocate?'" | "Says 'Can we revisit this next week?'" | "Talks with their mouth full." | "Complains about meeting fatigue." | "Shares an unrequested opinion." |
| "Forgets to turn their mic off after the meeting ends." | "Gets frustrated about a tech issue." | "Interrupts the host to go back to their point." | "Describes their home office setup." | "Says 'Let's workshop this.'" |

Name: _____

Date of meeting: _____

# Zoom Hog Bingo!

| | | | | |
|---|---|---|---|---|
| "Says 'Let's put a pin in this.'" | "Explains the same point three different ways." | "Talks about their weekend in detail." | "Starts a sentence with 'In my experience...'" | "Asks to reschedule partway through." |
| "Says 'I'm not sure this is relevant, but...'" | "Laughs awkwardly after a bad joke." | "Says 'Just to piggyback on that...'" | "Asks for everyone's opinion on a minor issue." | "Rants about a minor issue." |
| "Gets frustrated about a tech issue." | "Leaves their mic on during private conversation." | "Requests the host to extend the meeting." | "Has their pet make a cameo on-screen." | "Mentions how much coffee they've had." |
| "Uses the phrase 'going forward.'" | "Uses jargon no one understands." | "Tells a story no one asked for." | "Requests to 'table this discussion.'" | "Keeps asking for more examples." |
| "Says 'Can you email me the notes?'" | Free | "Uses 'at the end of the day' excessively." | "Forgets they're muted when starting a long sentence." | "Complains about their kids being noisy." |

Name: _____

Date of meeting: _____

# Zoom Hog Bingo!

| | | | | |
|---|---|---|---|---|
| "Complains about the time of the meeting." | "Gives an overly detailed update." | "Says 'Can we take a step back for a second?'" | "Says 'Can you repeat that last part?'" | "Keeps calling the host by the wrong name." |
| "Says 'This is a silly question, but...'" | "Takes a phone call during the meeting." | "Asks 'Is everyone still here?'" | "Takes the discussion way off-topic." | "Forgets to share their screen properly." |
| "Suggests splitting into another meeting." | "Asks if everyone can see their screen." | "Asks for a topic to be discussed again." | "Uses a fun filter, like cat ears." | "Mutes and unmutes repeatedly." |
| "Clicks their pen loudly." | "Requests to stay longer after the meeting ends." | "Mentions the weather." | "Tries to explain technical issues in detail." | "Eats loudly during the call." |
| "Mentions their upcoming vacation." | "Talks about a personal problem." | "Loses their train of thought mid-sentence." | Free | "Says 'Let me circle back to that.'" |

Name: _____

Date of meeting: _____

# Zoom Hog Bingo!

| | | | | |
|---|---|---|---|---|
| "Asks if this meeting is being recorded." | "Says 'I'll email you later about this.'" | "Talks to someone off-screen during the call." | "Claims they didn't get the agenda." | "Repeats the same question multiple times." |
| "Talks about lunch plans." | "Mentions how tired they are." | "Complains about their camera not working." | "Explains something already covered." | "Joins from their car." |
| "Interrupts to say 'Let me rephrase that.'" | "Mentions their bad internet connection." | "Shares their screen without warning." | Free | "Uses a distracting virtual background." |
| "Uses 'umm' excessively." | "Says 'This will only take a minute.'" | "Mentions how busy they are." | "Starts with 'This might be a stupid question, but...'" | "Talks over the host." |
| "Has loud background noise." | "Cracks an awkward joke that no one laughs at." | "Turns off their camera mid-meeting." | "Asks for a poll to be done." | "Overexplains their point." |

Name: _____

Date of meeting: _____

# Zoom Hog Bingo!

| "Mentions their weekend plans." | "Says 'Just one more question.'" | "Suggests scheduling a follow-up meeting." | "Forgets to unmute before talking." | "Complains about technical difficulties." |
|---|---|---|---|---|
| "I know we're over time, but..." | Free | "Uses the word 'synergy' or 'circle back.'" | "Sorry, I didn't catch that—can you repeat it?" | "Thanks everyone at least three times." |
| "Let me just add one quick point." | "Talks about something unrelated to work." | "Asks for the slides or notes to be sent after the meeting." | "Repeats what someone else just said." | "Interrupts the speaker to make a point." |
| "Says 'Can everyone hear me?'" | "Joins late and asks to recap everything." | "Mentions their pet or child during the call." | "Asks a question unrelated to the topic." | "Talks over someone else." |
| "Goes on a long personal anecdote." | "Keeps their camera off and only chimes in to talk." | "Says 'I'll keep this brief' but doesn't." | "Can we circle back to what I said earlier?" | "Asks for clarification after it was explained." |

Name: _____

Date of meeting: _____

# Zoom Hog Bingo!

| | | | | |
|---|---|---|---|---|
| "Asks for input after everyone has already shared." | "Doesn't realize their camera is on." | "Argues over the meeting's purpose." | "Turns the camera off without explanation." | "Talks about their workout routine." |
| "Refers to an email no one has seen." | "Says 'I'll just follow up later.'" | Free | "Says 'This is off-topic, but...'" | "Blames their tech issues on the software." |
| "Asks for slides mid-meeting." | "Has kids running in the background." | "Complains about the meeting length." | "Asks to 'circle back to that later.'" | "Says 'Can we take a quick break?'" |
| "Says 'Can I play devil's advocate?'" | "Says 'Can we revisit this next week?'" | "Talks with their mouth full." | "Complains about meeting fatigue." | "Shares an unrequested opinion." |
| "Forgets to turn their mic off after the meeting ends." | "Gets frustrated about a tech issue." | "Interrupts the host to go back to their point." | "Describes their home office setup." | "Says 'Let's workshop this.'" |

Name: _____

Date of meeting: _____

# Zoom Hog Bingo!

| "Says 'Let's put a pin in this.'" | "Explains the same point three different ways." | "Talks about their weekend in detail." | "Starts a sentence with 'In my experience...'" | "Asks to reschedule partway through." |
|---|---|---|---|---|
| "Says 'I'm not sure this is relevant, but...'" | "Laughs awkwardly after a bad joke." | "Says 'Just to piggyback on that...'" | "Asks for everyone's opinion on a minor issue." | "Rants about a minor issue." |
| "Gets frustrated about a tech issue." | "Leaves their mic on during private conversation." | "Requests the host to extend the meeting." | "Has their pet make a cameo on-screen." | "Mentions how much coffee they've had." |
| "Uses the phrase 'going forward.'" | "Uses jargon no one understands." | "Tells a story no one asked for." | "Requests to 'table this discussion.'" | "Keeps asking for more examples." |
| "Says 'Can you email me the notes?'" | Free | "Uses 'at the end of the day' excessively." | "Forgets they're muted when starting a long sentence." | "Complains about their kids being noisy." |

Name: _____

Date of meeting: _____

# Zoom Hog Bingo!

| | | | | |
|---|---|---|---|---|
| "Complains about the time of the meeting." | "Gives an overly detailed update." | "Says 'Can we take a step back for a second?'" | "Says 'Can you repeat that last part?'" | "Keeps calling the host by the wrong name." |
| "Says 'This is a silly question, but...'" | "Takes a phone call during the meeting." | "Asks 'Is everyone still here?'" | "Takes the discussion way off-topic." | "Forgets to share their screen properly." |
| "Suggests splitting into another meeting." | "Asks if everyone can see their screen." | "Asks for a topic to be discussed again." | "Uses a fun filter, like cat ears." | "Mutes and unmutes repeatedly." |
| "Clicks their pen loudly." | "Requests to stay longer after the meeting ends." | "Mentions the weather." | "Tries to explain technical issues in detail." | "Eats loudly during the call." |
| "Mentions their upcoming vacation." | "Talks about a personal problem." | "Loses their train of thought mid-sentence." | Free | "Says 'Let me circle back to that.'" |

Name: _____

Date of meeting: _____

# Zoom Hog Bingo!

| | | | | |
|---|---|---|---|---|
| "Asks if this meeting is being recorded." | "Says 'I'll email you later about this.'" | "Talks to someone off-screen during the call." | "Claims they didn't get the agenda." | "Repeats the same question multiple times." |
| "Talks about lunch plans." | "Mentions how tired they are." | "Complains about their camera not working." | "Explains something already covered." | "Joins from their car." |
| "Interrupts to say 'Let me rephrase that.'" | "Mentions their bad internet connection." | "Shares their screen without warning." | Free | "Uses a distracting virtual background." |
| "Uses 'umm' excessively." | "Says 'This will only take a minute.'" | "Mentions how busy they are." | "Starts with 'This might be a stupid question, but...'" | "Talks over the host." |
| "Has loud background noise." | "Cracks an awkward joke that no one laughs at." | "Turns off their camera mid-meeting." | "Asks for a poll to be done." | "Overexplains their point." |

Name: _____

Date of meeting: _____

# Zoom Hog Bingo!

| | | | | |
|---|---|---|---|---|
| "Mentions their weekend plans." | "Says 'Just one more question.'" | "Suggests scheduling a follow-up meeting." | "Forgets to unmute before talking." | "Complains about technical difficulties." |
| "I know we're over time, but..." | Free | "Uses the word 'synergy' or 'circle back.'" | "Sorry, I didn't catch that—can you repeat it?" | "Thanks everyone at least three times." |
| "Let me just add one quick point." | "Talks about something unrelated to work." | "Asks for the slides or notes to be sent after the meeting." | "Repeats what someone else just said." | "Interrupts the speaker to make a point." |
| "Says 'Can everyone hear me?'" | "Joins late and asks to recap everything." | "Mentions their pet or child during the call." | "Asks a question unrelated to the topic." | "Talks over someone else." |
| "Goes on a long personal anecdote." | "Keeps their camera off and only chimes in to talk." | "Says 'I'll keep this brief' but doesn't." | "Can we circle back to what I said earlier?" | "Asks for clarification after it was explained." |

Name: _____

Date of meeting: _____

# Zoom Hog Bingo!

| | | | | |
|---|---|---|---|---|
| "Asks for input after everyone has already shared." | "Doesn't realize their camera is on." | "Argues over the meeting's purpose." | "Turns the camera off without explanation." | "Talks about their workout routine." |
| "Refers to an email no one has seen." | "Says 'I'll just follow up later.'" | Free | "Says 'This is off-topic, but...'" | "Blames their tech issues on the software." |
| "Asks for slides mid-meeting." | "Has kids running in the background." | "Complains about the meeting length." | "Asks to 'circle back to that later.'" | "Says 'Can we take a quick break?'" |
| "Says 'Can I play devil's advocate?'" | "Says 'Can we revisit this next week?'" | "Talks with their mouth full." | "Complains about meeting fatigue." | "Shares an unrequested opinion." |
| "Forgets to turn their mic off after the meeting ends." | "Gets frustrated about a tech issue." | "Interrupts the host to go back to their point." | "Describes their home office setup." | "Says 'Let's workshop this.'" |

Name: _____

Date of meeting: _____

# Zoom Hog Bingo!

| | | | | |
|---|---|---|---|---|
| "Says 'Let's put a pin in this.'" | "Explains the same point three different ways." | "Talks about their weekend in detail." | "Starts a sentence with 'In my experience...'" | "Asks to reschedule partway through." |
| "Says 'I'm not sure this is relevant, but...'" | "Laughs awkwardly after a bad joke." | "Says 'Just to piggyback on that...'" | "Asks for everyone's opinion on a minor issue." | "Rants about a minor issue." |
| "Gets frustrated about a tech issue." | "Leaves their mic on during private conversation." | "Requests the host to extend the meeting." | "Has their pet make a cameo on-screen." | "Mentions how much coffee they've had." |
| "Uses the phrase 'going forward.'" | "Uses jargon no one understands." | "Tells a story no one asked for." | "Requests to 'table this discussion.'" | "Keeps asking for more examples." |
| "Says 'Can you email me the notes?'" | Free | "Uses 'at the end of the day' excessively." | "Forgets they're muted when starting a long sentence." | "Complains about their kids being noisy." |

Name: _____

Date of meeting: _____

# Zoom Hog Bingo!

| | | | | |
|---|---|---|---|---|
| "Complains about the time of the meeting." | "Gives an overly detailed update." | "Says 'Can we take a step back for a second?'" | "Says 'Can you repeat that last part?'" | "Keeps calling the host by the wrong name." |
| "Says 'This is a silly question, but...'" | "Takes a phone call during the meeting." | "Asks 'Is everyone still here?'" | "Takes the discussion way off-topic." | "Forgets to share their screen properly." |
| "Suggests splitting into another meeting." | "Asks if everyone can see their screen." | "Asks for a topic to be discussed again." | "Uses a fun filter, like cat ears." | "Mutes and unmutes repeatedly." |
| "Clicks their pen loudly." | "Requests to stay longer after the meeting ends." | "Mentions the weather." | "Tries to explain technical issues in detail." | "Eats loudly during the call." |
| "Mentions their upcoming vacation." | "Talks about a personal problem." | "Loses their train of thought mid-sentence." | Free | "Says 'Let me circle back to that.'" |

Name: _____

Date of meeting: _____

# Zoom Hog Bingo!

| | | | | |
|---|---|---|---|---|
| "Asks if this meeting is being recorded." | "Says 'I'll email you later about this.'" | "Talks to someone off-screen during the call." | "Claims they didn't get the agenda." | "Repeats the same question multiple times." |
| "Talks about lunch plans." | "Mentions how tired they are." | "Complains about their camera not working." | "Explains something already covered." | "Joins from their car." |
| "Interrupts to say 'Let me rephrase that.'" | "Mentions their bad internet connection." | "Shares their screen without warning." | Free | "Uses a distracting virtual background." |
| "Uses 'umm' excessively." | "Says 'This will only take a minute.'" | "Mentions how busy they are." | "Starts with 'This might be a stupid question, but...'" | "Talks over the host." |
| "Has loud background noise." | "Cracks an awkward joke that no one laughs at." | "Turns off their camera mid-meeting." | "Asks for a poll to be done." | "Overexplains their point." |

Name: _____

Date of meeting: _____

# Zoom Hog Bingo!

| | | | | |
|---|---|---|---|---|
| "Mentions their weekend plans." | "Says 'Just one more question.'" | "Suggests scheduling a follow-up meeting." | "Forgets to unmute before talking." | "Complains about technical difficulties." |
| "I know we're over time, but..." | Free | "Uses the word 'synergy' or 'circle back.'" | "Sorry, I didn't catch that—can you repeat it?" | "Thanks everyone at least three times." |
| "Let me just add one quick point." | "Talks about something unrelated to work." | "Asks for the slides or notes to be sent after the meeting." | "Repeats what someone else just said." | "Interrupts the speaker to make a point." |
| "Says 'Can everyone hear me?'" | "Joins late and asks to recap everything." | "Mentions their pet or child during the call." | "Asks a question unrelated to the topic." | "Talks over someone else." |
| "Goes on a long personal anecdote." | "Keeps their camera off and only chimes in to talk." | "Says 'I'll keep this brief' but doesn't." | "Can we circle back to what I said earlier?" | "Asks for clarification after it was explained." |

Name: _____

Date of meeting: _____

# Zoom Hog Bingo!

| | | | | |
|---|---|---|---|---|
| "Asks for input after everyone has already shared." | "Doesn't realize their camera is on." | "Argues over the meeting's purpose." | "Turns the camera off without explanation." | "Talks about their workout routine." |
| "Refers to an email no one has seen." | "Says 'I'll just follow up later.'" | Free | "Says 'This is off-topic, but...'" | "Blames their tech issues on the software." |
| "Asks for slides mid-meeting." | "Has kids running in the background." | "Complains about the meeting length." | "Asks to 'circle back to that later.'" | "Says 'Can we take a quick break?'" |
| "Says 'Can I play devil's advocate?'" | "Says 'Can we revisit this next week?'" | "Talks with their mouth full." | "Complains about meeting fatigue." | "Shares an unrequested opinion." |
| "Forgets to turn their mic off after the meeting ends." | "Gets frustrated about a tech issue." | "Interrupts the host to go back to their point." | "Describes their home office setup." | "Says 'Let's workshop this.'" |

Name: _____

Date of meeting: _____

# Zoom Hog Bingo!

| | | | | |
|---|---|---|---|---|
| "Says 'Let's put a pin in this.'" | "Explains the same point three different ways." | "Talks about their weekend in detail." | "Starts a sentence with 'In my experience...'" | "Asks to reschedule partway through." |
| "Says 'I'm not sure this is relevant, but...'" | "Laughs awkwardly after a bad joke." | "Says 'Just to piggyback on that...'" | "Asks for everyone's opinion on a minor issue." | "Rants about a minor issue." |
| "Gets frustrated about a tech issue." | "Leaves their mic on during private conversation." | "Requests the host to extend the meeting." | "Has their pet make a cameo on-screen." | "Mentions how much coffee they've had." |
| "Uses the phrase 'going forward.'" | "Uses jargon no one understands." | "Tells a story no one asked for." | "Requests to 'table this discussion.'" | "Keeps asking for more examples." |
| "Says 'Can you email me the notes?'" | Free | "Uses 'at the end of the day' excessively." | "Forgets they're muted when starting a long sentence." | "Complains about their kids being noisy." |

Name: _____

Date of meeting: _____

# Zoom Hog Bingo!

| | | | | |
|---|---|---|---|---|
| "Complains about the time of the meeting." | "Gives an overly detailed update." | "Says 'Can we take a step back for a second?'" | "Says 'Can you repeat that last part?'" | "Keeps calling the host by the wrong name." |
| "Says 'This is a silly question, but...'" | "Takes a phone call during the meeting." | "Asks 'Is everyone still here?'" | "Takes the discussion way off-topic." | "Forgets to share their screen properly." |
| "Suggests splitting into another meeting." | "Asks if everyone can see their screen." | "Asks for a topic to be discussed again." | "Uses a fun filter, like cat ears." | "Mutes and unmutes repeatedly." |
| "Clicks their pen loudly." | "Requests to stay longer after the meeting ends." | "Mentions the weather." | "Tries to explain technical issues in detail." | "Eats loudly during the call." |
| "Mentions their upcoming vacation." | "Talks about a personal problem." | "Loses their train of thought mid-sentence." | Free | "Says 'Let me circle back to that.'" |

Name: _____

Date of meeting: _____

# Zoom Hog Bingo!

| | | | | |
|---|---|---|---|---|
| "Asks if this meeting is being recorded." | "Says 'I'll email you later about this.'" | "Talks to someone off-screen during the call." | "Claims they didn't get the agenda." | "Repeats the same question multiple times." |
| "Talks about lunch plans." | "Mentions how tired they are." | "Complains about their camera not working." | "Explains something already covered." | "Joins from their car." |
| "Interrupts to say 'Let me rephrase that.'" | "Mentions their bad internet connection." | "Shares their screen without warning." | Free | "Uses a distracting virtual background." |
| "Uses 'umm' excessively." | "Says 'This will only take a minute.'" | "Mentions how busy they are." | "Starts with 'This might be a stupid question, but...'" | "Talks over the host." |
| "Has loud background noise." | "Cracks an awkward joke that no one laughs at." | "Turns off their camera mid-meeting." | "Asks for a poll to be done." | "Overexplains their point." |

Name: _____

Date of meeting: _____

# Zoom Hog Bingo!

| "Mentions their weekend plans." | "Says 'Just one more question.'" | "Suggests scheduling a follow-up meeting." | "Forgets to unmute before talking." | "Complains about technical difficulties." |
|---|---|---|---|---|
| "I know we're over time, but..." | Free | "Uses the word 'synergy' or 'circle back.'" | "Sorry, I didn't catch that—can you repeat it?" | "Thanks everyone at least three times." |
| "Let me just add one quick point." | "Talks about something unrelated to work." | "Asks for the slides or notes to be sent after the meeting." | "Repeats what someone else just said." | "Interrupts the speaker to make a point." |
| "Says 'Can everyone hear me?'" | "Joins late and asks to recap everything." | "Mentions their pet or child during the call." | "Asks a question unrelated to the topic." | "Talks over someone else." |
| "Goes on a long personal anecdote." | "Keeps their camera off and only chimes in to talk." | "Says 'I'll keep this brief' but doesn't." | "Can we circle back to what I said earlier?" | "Asks for clarification after it was explained." |

Name: _____

Date of meeting: _____

# Zoom Hog Bingo!

| | | | | |
|---|---|---|---|---|
| "Asks for input after everyone has already shared." | "Doesn't realize their camera is on." | "Argues over the meeting's purpose." | "Turns the camera off without explanation." | "Talks about their workout routine." |
| "Refers to an email no one has seen." | "Says 'I'll just follow up later.'" | Free | "Says 'This is off-topic, but...'" | "Blames their tech issues on the software." |
| "Asks for slides mid-meeting." | "Has kids running in the background." | "Complains about the meeting length." | "Asks to 'circle back to that later.'" | "Says 'Can we take a quick break?'" |
| "Says 'Can I play devil's advocate?'" | "Says 'Can we revisit this next week?'" | "Talks with their mouth full." | "Complains about meeting fatigue." | "Shares an unrequested opinion." |
| "Forgets to turn their mic off after the meeting ends." | "Gets frustrated about a tech issue." | "Interrupts the host to go back to their point." | "Describes their home office setup." | "Says 'Let's workshop this.'" |

Name: _____

Date of meeting: _____

# Zoom Hog Bingo!

| | | | | |
|---|---|---|---|---|
| "Says 'Let's put a pin in this.'" | "Explains the same point three different ways." | "Talks about their weekend in detail." | "Starts a sentence with 'In my experience...'" | "Asks to reschedule partway through." |
| "Says 'I'm not sure this is relevant, but...'" | "Laughs awkwardly after a bad joke." | "Says 'Just to piggyback on that...'" | "Asks for everyone's opinion on a minor issue." | "Rants about a minor issue." |
| "Gets frustrated about a tech issue." | "Leaves their mic on during private conversation." | "Requests the host to extend the meeting." | "Has their pet make a cameo on-screen." | "Mentions how much coffee they've had." |
| "Uses the phrase 'going forward.'" | "Uses jargon no one understands." | "Tells a story no one asked for." | "Requests to 'table this discussion.'" | "Keeps asking for more examples." |
| "Says 'Can you email me the notes?'" | Free | "Uses 'at the end of the day' excessively." | "Forgets they're muted when starting a long sentence." | "Complains about their kids being noisy." |

Name: _____

Date of meeting: _____

# Zoom Hog Bingo!

| | | | | |
|---|---|---|---|---|
| "Complains about the time of the meeting." | "Gives an overly detailed update." | "Says 'Can we take a step back for a second?'" | "Says 'Can you repeat that last part?'" | "Keeps calling the host by the wrong name." |
| "Says 'This is a silly question, but...'" | "Takes a phone call during the meeting." | "Asks 'Is everyone still here?'" | "Takes the discussion way off-topic." | "Forgets to share their screen properly." |
| "Suggests splitting into another meeting." | "Asks if everyone can see their screen." | "Asks for a topic to be discussed again." | "Uses a fun filter, like cat ears." | "Mutes and unmutes repeatedly." |
| "Clicks their pen loudly." | "Requests to stay longer after the meeting ends." | "Mentions the weather." | "Tries to explain technical issues in detail." | "Eats loudly during the call." |
| "Mentions their upcoming vacation." | "Talks about a personal problem." | "Loses their train of thought mid-sentence." | Free | "Says 'Let me circle back to that.'" |

Name: _____

Date of meeting: _____

# Zoom Hog Bingo!

| | | | | |
|---|---|---|---|---|
| "Asks if this meeting is being recorded." | "Says 'I'll email you later about this.'" | "Talks to someone off-screen during the call." | "Claims they didn't get the agenda." | "Repeats the same question multiple times." |
| "Talks about lunch plans." | "Mentions how tired they are." | "Complains about their camera not working." | "Explains something already covered." | "Joins from their car." |
| "Interrupts to say 'Let me rephrase that.'" | "Mentions their bad internet connection." | "Shares their screen without warning." | Free | "Uses a distracting virtual background." |
| "Uses 'umm' excessively." | "Says 'This will only take a minute.'" | "Mentions how busy they are." | "Starts with 'This might be a stupid question, but...'" | "Talks over the host." |
| "Has loud background noise." | "Cracks an awkward joke that no one laughs at." | "Turns off their camera mid-meeting." | "Asks for a poll to be done." | "Overexplains their point." |

Name: _____

Date of meeting: _____

# Zoom Hog Bingo!

| | | | | |
|---|---|---|---|---|
| "Mentions their weekend plans." | "Says 'Just one more question.'" | "Suggests scheduling a follow-up meeting." | "Forgets to unmute before talking." | "Complains about technical difficulties." |
| "I know we're over time, but..." | Free | "Uses the word 'synergy' or 'circle back.'" | "Sorry, I didn't catch that—can you repeat it?" | "Thanks everyone at least three times." |
| "Let me just add one quick point." | "Talks about something unrelated to work." | "Asks for the slides or notes to be sent after the meeting." | "Repeats what someone else just said." | "Interrupts the speaker to make a point." |
| "Says 'Can everyone hear me?'" | "Joins late and asks to recap everything." | "Mentions their pet or child during the call." | "Asks a question unrelated to the topic." | "Talks over someone else." |
| "Goes on a long personal anecdote." | "Keeps their camera off and only chimes in to talk." | "Says 'I'll keep this brief' but doesn't." | "Can we circle back to what I said earlier?" | "Asks for clarification after it was explained." |

Name: _____

Date of meeting: _____

# Zoom Hog Bingo!

| | | | | |
|---|---|---|---|---|
| "Asks for input after everyone has already shared." | "Doesn't realize their camera is on." | "Argues over the meeting's purpose." | "Turns the camera off without explanation." | "Talks about their workout routine." |
| "Refers to an email no one has seen." | "Says 'I'll just follow up later.'" | Free | "Says 'This is off-topic, but...'" | "Blames their tech issues on the software." |
| "Asks for slides mid-meeting." | "Has kids running in the background." | "Complains about the meeting length." | "Asks to 'circle back to that later.'" | "Says 'Can we take a quick break?'" |
| "Says 'Can I play devil's advocate?'" | "Says 'Can we revisit this next week?'" | "Talks with their mouth full." | "Complains about meeting fatigue." | "Shares an unrequested opinion." |
| "Forgets to turn their mic off after the meeting ends." | "Gets frustrated about a tech issue." | "Interrupts the host to go back to their point." | "Describes their home office setup." | "Says 'Let's workshop this.'" |

Name: _____

Date of meeting: _____

# Zoom Hog Bingo!

| | | | | |
|---|---|---|---|---|
| "Says 'Let's put a pin in this.'" | "Explains the same point three different ways." | "Talks about their weekend in detail." | "Starts a sentence with 'In my experience...'" | "Asks to reschedule partway through." |
| "Says 'I'm not sure this is relevant, but...'" | "Laughs awkwardly after a bad joke." | "Says 'Just to piggyback on that...'" | "Asks for everyone's opinion on a minor issue." | "Rants about a minor issue." |
| "Gets frustrated about a tech issue." | "Leaves their mic on during private conversation." | "Requests the host to extend the meeting." | "Has their pet make a cameo on-screen." | "Mentions how much coffee they've had." |
| "Uses the phrase 'going forward.'" | "Uses jargon no one understands." | "Tells a story no one asked for." | "Requests to 'table this discussion.'" | "Keeps asking for more examples." |
| "Says 'Can you email me the notes?'" | Free | "Uses 'at the end of the day' excessively." | "Forgets they're muted when starting a long sentence." | "Complains about their kids being noisy." |

Name: _____

Date of meeting: _____

# Zoom Hog Bingo!

| | | | | |
|---|---|---|---|---|
| "Complains about the time of the meeting." | "Gives an overly detailed update." | "Says 'Can we take a step back for a second?'" | "Says 'Can you repeat that last part?'" | "Keeps calling the host by the wrong name." |
| "Says 'This is a silly question, but...'" | "Takes a phone call during the meeting." | "Asks 'Is everyone still here?'" | "Takes the discussion way off-topic." | "Forgets to share their screen properly." |
| "Suggests splitting into another meeting." | "Asks if everyone can see their screen." | "Asks for a topic to be discussed again." | "Uses a fun filter, like cat ears." | "Mutes and unmutes repeatedly." |
| "Clicks their pen loudly." | "Requests to stay longer after the meeting ends." | "Mentions the weather." | "Tries to explain technical issues in detail." | "Eats loudly during the call." |
| "Mentions their upcoming vacation." | "Talks about a personal problem." | "Loses their train of thought mid-sentence." | Free | "Says 'Let me circle back to that.'" |

Name: _____

Date of meeting: _____

# Zoom Hog Bingo!

| | | | | |
|---|---|---|---|---|
| "Asks if this meeting is being recorded." | "Says 'I'll email you later about this.'" | "Talks to someone off-screen during the call." | "Claims they didn't get the agenda." | "Repeats the same question multiple times." |
| "Talks about lunch plans." | "Mentions how tired they are." | "Complains about their camera not working." | "Explains something already covered." | "Joins from their car." |
| "Interrupts to say 'Let me rephrase that.'" | "Mentions their bad internet connection." | "Shares their screen without warning." | Free | "Uses a distracting virtual background." |
| "Uses 'umm' excessively." | "Says 'This will only take a minute.'" | "Mentions how busy they are." | "Starts with 'This might be a stupid question, but...'" | "Talks over the host." |
| "Has loud background noise." | "Cracks an awkward joke that no one laughs at." | "Turns off their camera mid-meeting." | "Asks for a poll to be done." | "Overexplains their point." |

Name: _____

Date of meeting: _____

# Zoom Hog Bingo!

| | | | | |
|---|---|---|---|---|
| "Mentions their weekend plans." | "Says 'Just one more question.'" | "Suggests scheduling a follow-up meeting." | "Forgets to unmute before talking." | "Complains about technical difficulties." |
| "I know we're over time, but..." | Free | "Uses the word 'synergy' or 'circle back.'" | "Sorry, I didn't catch that—can you repeat it?" | "Thanks everyone at least three times." |
| "Let me just add one quick point." | "Talks about something unrelated to work." | "Asks for the slides or notes to be sent after the meeting." | "Repeats what someone else just said." | "Interrupts the speaker to make a point." |
| "Says 'Can everyone hear me?'" | "Joins late and asks to recap everything." | "Mentions their pet or child during the call." | "Asks a question unrelated to the topic." | "Talks over someone else." |
| "Goes on a long personal anecdote." | "Keeps their camera off and only chimes in to talk." | "Says 'I'll keep this brief' but doesn't." | "Can we circle back to what I said earlier?" | "Asks for clarification after it was explained." |

Name: _____

Date of meeting: _____

# Zoom Hog Bingo!

| | | | | |
|---|---|---|---|---|
| "Asks for input after everyone has already shared." | "Doesn't realize their camera is on." | "Argues over the meeting's purpose." | "Turns the camera off without explanation." | "Talks about their workout routine." |
| "Refers to an email no one has seen." | "Says 'I'll just follow up later.'" | Free | "Says 'This is off-topic, but...'" | "Blames their tech issues on the software." |
| "Asks for slides mid-meeting." | "Has kids running in the background." | "Complains about the meeting length." | "Asks to 'circle back to that later.'" | "Says 'Can we take a quick break?'" |
| "Says 'Can I play devil's advocate?'" | "Says 'Can we revisit this next week?'" | "Talks with their mouth full." | "Complains about meeting fatigue." | "Shares an unrequested opinion." |
| "Forgets to turn their mic off after the meeting ends." | "Gets frustrated about a tech issue." | "Interrupts the host to go back to their point." | "Describes their home office setup." | "Says 'Let's workshop this.'" |

Name: _____

Date of meeting: _____

# Zoom Hog Bingo!

| | | | | |
|---|---|---|---|---|
| "Says 'Let's put a pin in this.'" | "Explains the same point three different ways." | "Talks about their weekend in detail." | "Starts a sentence with 'In my experience...'" | "Asks to reschedule partway through." |
| "Says 'I'm not sure this is relevant, but...'" | "Laughs awkwardly after a bad joke." | "Says 'Just to piggyback on that...'" | "Asks for everyone's opinion on a minor issue." | "Rants about a minor issue." |
| "Gets frustrated about a tech issue." | "Leaves their mic on during private conversation." | "Requests the host to extend the meeting." | "Has their pet make a cameo on-screen." | "Mentions how much coffee they've had." |
| "Uses the phrase 'going forward.'" | "Uses jargon no one understands." | "Tells a story no one asked for." | "Requests to 'table this discussion.'" | "Keeps asking for more examples." |
| "Says 'Can you email me the notes?'" | Free | "Uses 'at the end of the day' excessively." | "Forgets they're muted when starting a long sentence." | "Complains about their kids being noisy." |

Name: _____

Date of meeting: _____

# Zoom Hog Bingo!

| | | | | |
|---|---|---|---|---|
| "Complains about the time of the meeting." | "Gives an overly detailed update." | "Says 'Can we take a step back for a second?'" | "Says 'Can you repeat that last part?'" | "Keeps calling the host by the wrong name." |
| "Says 'This is a silly question, but...'" | "Takes a phone call during the meeting." | "Asks 'Is everyone still here?'" | "Takes the discussion way off-topic." | "Forgets to share their screen properly." |
| "Suggests splitting into another meeting." | "Asks if everyone can see their screen." | "Asks for a topic to be discussed again." | "Uses a fun filter, like cat ears." | "Mutes and unmutes repeatedly." |
| "Clicks their pen loudly." | "Requests to stay longer after the meeting ends." | "Mentions the weather." | "Tries to explain technical issues in detail." | "Eats loudly during the call." |
| "Mentions their upcoming vacation." | "Talks about a personal problem." | "Loses their train of thought mid-sentence." | Free | "Says 'Let me circle back to that.'" |

Name: _____

Date of meeting: _____

# Zoom Hog Bingo!

| | | | | |
|---|---|---|---|---|
| "Asks if this meeting is being recorded." | "Says 'I'll email you later about this.'" | "Talks to someone off-screen during the call." | "Claims they didn't get the agenda." | "Repeats the same question multiple times." |
| "Talks about lunch plans." | "Mentions how tired they are." | "Complains about their camera not working." | "Explains something already covered." | "Joins from their car." |
| "Interrupts to say 'Let me rephrase that.'" | "Mentions their bad internet connection." | "Shares their screen without warning." | Free | "Uses a distracting virtual background." |
| "Uses 'umm' excessively." | "Says 'This will only take a minute.'" | "Mentions how busy they are." | "Starts with 'This might be a stupid question, but...'" | "Talks over the host." |
| "Has loud background noise." | "Cracks an awkward joke that no one laughs at." | "Turns off their camera mid-meeting." | "Asks for a poll to be done." | "Overexplains their point." |

Name: _____

Date of meeting: _____

# Zoom Hog Bingo!

| | | | | |
|---|---|---|---|---|
| "Mentions their weekend plans." | "Says 'Just one more question.'" | "Suggests scheduling a follow-up meeting." | "Forgets to unmute before talking." | "Complains about technical difficulties." |
| "I know we're over time, but..." | Free | "Uses the word 'synergy' or 'circle back.'" | "Sorry, I didn't catch that—can you repeat it?" | "Thanks everyone at least three times." |
| "Let me just add one quick point." | "Talks about something unrelated to work." | "Asks for the slides or notes to be sent after the meeting." | "Repeats what someone else just said." | "Interrupts the speaker to make a point." |
| "Says 'Can everyone hear me?'" | "Joins late and asks to recap everything." | "Mentions their pet or child during the call." | "Asks a question unrelated to the topic." | "Talks over someone else." |
| "Goes on a long personal anecdote." | "Keeps their camera off and only chimes in to talk." | "Says 'I'll keep this brief' but doesn't." | "Can we circle back to what I said earlier?" | "Asks for clarification after it was explained." |

Name: _____

Date of meeting: _____

# Zoom Hog Bingo!

| | | | | |
|---|---|---|---|---|
| "Asks for input after everyone has already shared." | "Doesn't realize their camera is on." | "Argues over the meeting's purpose." | "Turns the camera off without explanation." | "Talks about their workout routine." |
| "Refers to an email no one has seen." | "Says 'I'll just follow up later.'" | Free | "Says 'This is off-topic, but...'" | "Blames their tech issues on the software." |
| "Asks for slides mid-meeting." | "Has kids running in the background." | "Complains about the meeting length." | "Asks to 'circle back to that later.'" | "Says 'Can we take a quick break?'" |
| "Says 'Can I play devil's advocate?'" | "Says 'Can we revisit this next week?'" | "Talks with their mouth full." | "Complains about meeting fatigue." | "Shares an unrequested opinion." |
| "Forgets to turn their mic off after the meeting ends." | "Gets frustrated about a tech issue." | "Interrupts the host to go back to their point." | "Describes their home office setup." | "Says 'Let's workshop this.'" |

Name: _____

Date of meeting: _____

# Zoom Hog Bingo!

| | | | | |
|---|---|---|---|---|
| "Says 'Let's put a pin in this.'" | "Explains the same point three different ways." | "Talks about their weekend in detail." | "Starts a sentence with 'In my experience...'" | "Asks to reschedule partway through." |
| "Says 'I'm not sure this is relevant, but...'" | "Laughs awkwardly after a bad joke." | "Says 'Just to piggyback on that...'" | "Asks for everyone's opinion on a minor issue." | "Rants about a minor issue." |
| "Gets frustrated about a tech issue." | "Leaves their mic on during private conversation." | "Requests the host to extend the meeting." | "Has their pet make a cameo on-screen." | "Mentions how much coffee they've had." |
| "Uses the phrase 'going forward.'" | "Uses jargon no one understands." | "Tells a story no one asked for." | "Requests to 'table this discussion.'" | "Keeps asking for more examples." |
| "Says 'Can you email me the notes?'" | Free | "Uses 'at the end of the day' excessively." | "Forgets they're muted when starting a long sentence." | "Complains about their kids being noisy." |

Name: _____

Date of meeting: _____

# Zoom Hog Bingo!

| | | | | |
|---|---|---|---|---|
| "Complains about the time of the meeting." | "Gives an overly detailed update." | "Says 'Can we take a step back for a second?'" | "Says 'Can you repeat that last part?'" | "Keeps calling the host by the wrong name." |
| "Says 'This is a silly question, but...'" | "Takes a phone call during the meeting." | "Asks 'Is everyone still here?'" | "Takes the discussion way off-topic." | "Forgets to share their screen properly." |
| "Suggests splitting into another meeting." | "Asks if everyone can see their screen." | "Asks for a topic to be discussed again." | "Uses a fun filter, like cat ears." | "Mutes and unmutes repeatedly." |
| "Clicks their pen loudly." | "Requests to stay longer after the meeting ends." | "Mentions the weather." | "Tries to explain technical issues in detail." | "Eats loudly during the call." |
| "Mentions their upcoming vacation." | "Talks about a personal problem." | "Loses their train of thought mid-sentence." | Free | "Says 'Let me circle back to that.'" |

Name: _____

Date of meeting: _____

# Zoom Hog Bingo!

| | | | | |
|---|---|---|---|---|
| "Asks if this meeting is being recorded." | "Says 'I'll email you later about this.'" | "Talks to someone off-screen during the call." | "Claims they didn't get the agenda." | "Repeats the same question multiple times." |
| "Talks about lunch plans." | "Mentions how tired they are." | "Complains about their camera not working." | "Explains something already covered." | "Joins from their car." |
| "Interrupts to say 'Let me rephrase that.'" | "Mentions their bad internet connection." | "Shares their screen without warning." | Free | "Uses a distracting virtual background." |
| "Uses 'umm' excessively." | "Says 'This will only take a minute.'" | "Mentions how busy they are." | "Starts with 'This might be a stupid question, but...'" | "Talks over the host." |
| "Has loud background noise." | "Cracks an awkward joke that no one laughs at." | "Turns off their camera mid-meeting." | "Asks for a poll to be done." | "Overexplains their point." |

Name: _____

Date of meeting: _____

# Zoom Hog Bingo!

| | | | | |
|---|---|---|---|---|
| "Mentions their weekend plans." | "Says 'Just one more question.'" | "Suggests scheduling a follow-up meeting." | "Forgets to unmute before talking." | "Complains about technical difficulties." |
| "I know we're over time, but..." | Free | "Uses the word 'synergy' or 'circle back.'" | "Sorry, I didn't catch that—can you repeat it?" | "Thanks everyone at least three times." |
| "Let me just add one quick point." | "Talks about something unrelated to work." | "Asks for the slides or notes to be sent after the meeting." | "Repeats what someone else just said." | "Interrupts the speaker to make a point." |
| "Says 'Can everyone hear me?'" | "Joins late and asks to recap everything." | "Mentions their pet or child during the call." | "Asks a question unrelated to the topic." | "Talks over someone else." |
| "Goes on a long personal anecdote." | "Keeps their camera off and only chimes in to talk." | "Says 'I'll keep this brief' but doesn't." | "Can we circle back to what I said earlier?" | "Asks for clarification after it was explained." |

Name: _____

Date of meeting: _____

# Zoom Hog Bingo!

| | | | | |
|---|---|---|---|---|
| "Asks for input after everyone has already shared." | "Doesn't realize their camera is on." | "Argues over the meeting's purpose." | "Turns the camera off without explanation." | "Talks about their workout routine." |
| "Refers to an email no one has seen." | "Says 'I'll just follow up later.'" | Free | "Says 'This is off-topic, but...'" | "Blames their tech issues on the software." |
| "Asks for slides mid-meeting." | "Has kids running in the background." | "Complains about the meeting length." | "Asks to 'circle back to that later.'" | "Says 'Can we take a quick break?'" |
| "Says 'Can I play devil's advocate?'" | "Says 'Can we revisit this next week?'" | "Talks with their mouth full." | "Complains about meeting fatigue." | "Shares an unrequested opinion." |
| "Forgets to turn their mic off after the meeting ends." | "Gets frustrated about a tech issue." | "Interrupts the host to go back to their point." | "Describes their home office setup." | "Says 'Let's workshop this.'" |

Name: _____

Date of meeting: _____

# Zoom Hog Bingo!

| | | | | |
|---|---|---|---|---|
| "Says 'Let's put a pin in this.'" | "Explains the same point three different ways." | "Talks about their weekend in detail." | "Starts a sentence with 'In my experience…'" | "Asks to reschedule partway through." |
| "Says 'I'm not sure this is relevant, but…'" | "Laughs awkwardly after a bad joke." | "Says 'Just to piggyback on that…'" | "Asks for everyone's opinion on a minor issue." | "Rants about a minor issue." |
| "Gets frustrated about a tech issue." | "Leaves their mic on during private conversation." | "Requests the host to extend the meeting." | "Has their pet make a cameo on-screen." | "Mentions how much coffee they've had." |
| "Uses the phrase 'going forward.'" | "Uses jargon no one understands." | "Tells a story no one asked for." | "Requests to 'table this discussion.'" | "Keeps asking for more examples." |
| "Says 'Can you email me the notes?'" | Free | "Uses 'at the end of the day' excessively." | "Forgets they're muted when starting a long sentence." | "Complains about their kids being noisy." |

Name: _____

Date of meeting: _____

# Zoom Hog Bingo!

| | | | | |
|---|---|---|---|---|
| "Complains about the time of the meeting." | "Gives an overly detailed update." | "Says 'Can we take a step back for a second?'" | "Says 'Can you repeat that last part?'" | "Keeps calling the host by the wrong name." |
| "Says 'This is a silly question, but...'" | "Takes a phone call during the meeting." | "Asks 'Is everyone still here?'" | "Takes the discussion way off-topic." | "Forgets to share their screen properly." |
| "Suggests splitting into another meeting." | "Asks if everyone can see their screen." | "Asks for a topic to be discussed again." | "Uses a fun filter, like cat ears." | "Mutes and unmutes repeatedly." |
| "Clicks their pen loudly." | "Requests to stay longer after the meeting ends." | "Mentions the weather." | "Tries to explain technical issues in detail." | "Eats loudly during the call." |
| "Mentions their upcoming vacation." | "Talks about a personal problem." | "Loses their train of thought mid-sentence." | Free | "Says 'Let me circle back to that.'" |

Name: _____

Date of meeting: _____

# Zoom Hog Bingo!

| | | | | |
|---|---|---|---|---|
| "Asks if this meeting is being recorded." | "Says 'I'll email you later about this.'" | "Talks to someone off-screen during the call." | "Claims they didn't get the agenda." | "Repeats the same question multiple times." |
| "Talks about lunch plans." | "Mentions how tired they are." | "Complains about their camera not working." | "Explains something already covered." | "Joins from their car." |
| "Interrupts to say 'Let me rephrase that.'" | "Mentions their bad internet connection." | "Shares their screen without warning." | Free | "Uses a distracting virtual background." |
| "Uses 'umm' excessively." | "Says 'This will only take a minute.'" | "Mentions how busy they are." | "Starts with 'This might be a stupid question, but...'" | "Talks over the host." |
| "Has loud background noise." | "Cracks an awkward joke that no one laughs at." | "Turns off their camera mid-meeting." | "Asks for a poll to be done." | "Overexplains their point." |

Name: _____

Date of meeting: _____

# Zoom Hog Bingo!

| | | | | |
|---|---|---|---|---|
| "Mentions their weekend plans." | "Says 'Just one more question.'" | "Suggests scheduling a follow-up meeting." | "Forgets to unmute before talking." | "Complains about technical difficulties." |
| "I know we're over time, but..." | Free | "Uses the word 'synergy' or 'circle back.'" | "Sorry, I didn't catch that—can you repeat it?" | "Thanks everyone at least three times." |
| "Let me just add one quick point." | "Talks about something unrelated to work." | "Asks for the slides or notes to be sent after the meeting." | "Repeats what someone else just said." | "Interrupts the speaker to make a point." |
| "Says 'Can everyone hear me?'" | "Joins late and asks to recap everything." | "Mentions their pet or child during the call." | "Asks a question unrelated to the topic." | "Talks over someone else." |
| "Goes on a long personal anecdote." | "Keeps their camera off and only chimes in to talk." | "Says 'I'll keep this brief' but doesn't." | "Can we circle back to what I said earlier?" | "Asks for clarification after it was explained." |

Name: _____

Date of meeting: _____

# Zoom Hog Bingo!

| | | | | |
|---|---|---|---|---|
| "Asks for input after everyone has already shared." | "Doesn't realize their camera is on." | "Argues over the meeting's purpose." | "Turns the camera off without explanation." | "Talks about their workout routine." |
| "Refers to an email no one has seen." | "Says 'I'll just follow up later.'" | Free | "Says 'This is off-topic, but...'" | "Blames their tech issues on the software." |
| "Asks for slides mid-meeting." | "Has kids running in the background." | "Complains about the meeting length." | "Asks to 'circle back to that later.'" | "Says 'Can we take a quick break?'" |
| "Says 'Can I play devil's advocate?'" | "Says 'Can we revisit this next week?'" | "Talks with their mouth full." | "Complains about meeting fatigue." | "Shares an unrequested opinion." |
| "Forgets to turn their mic off after the meeting ends." | "Gets frustrated about a tech issue." | "Interrupts the host to go back to their point." | "Describes their home office setup." | "Says 'Let's workshop this.'" |

Name: _____

Date of meeting: _____

# Zoom Hog Bingo!

| | | | | |
|---|---|---|---|---|
| "Says 'Let's put a pin in this.'" | "Explains the same point three different ways." | "Talks about their weekend in detail." | "Starts a sentence with 'In my experience...'" | "Asks to reschedule partway through." |
| "Says 'I'm not sure this is relevant, but...'" | "Laughs awkwardly after a bad joke." | "Says 'Just to piggyback on that...'" | "Asks for everyone's opinion on a minor issue." | "Rants about a minor issue." |
| "Gets frustrated about a tech issue." | "Leaves their mic on during private conversation." | "Requests the host to extend the meeting." | "Has their pet make a cameo on-screen." | "Mentions how much coffee they've had." |
| "Uses the phrase 'going forward.'" | "Uses jargon no one understands." | "Tells a story no one asked for." | "Requests to 'table this discussion.'" | "Keeps asking for more examples." |
| "Says 'Can you email me the notes?'" | Free | "Uses 'at the end of the day' excessively." | "Forgets they're muted when starting a long sentence." | "Complains about their kids being noisy." |

Name: _____

Date of meeting: _____

# Zoom Hog Bingo!

| | | | | |
|---|---|---|---|---|
| "Complains about the time of the meeting." | "Gives an overly detailed update." | "Says 'Can we take a step back for a second?'" | "Says 'Can you repeat that last part?'" | "Keeps calling the host by the wrong name." |
| "Says 'This is a silly question, but...'" | "Takes a phone call during the meeting." | "Asks 'Is everyone still here?'" | "Takes the discussion way off-topic." | "Forgets to share their screen properly." |
| "Suggests splitting into another meeting." | "Asks if everyone can see their screen." | "Asks for a topic to be discussed again." | "Uses a fun filter, like cat ears." | "Mutes and unmutes repeatedly." |
| "Clicks their pen loudly." | "Requests to stay longer after the meeting ends." | "Mentions the weather." | "Tries to explain technical issues in detail." | "Eats loudly during the call." |
| "Mentions their upcoming vacation." | "Talks about a personal problem." | "Loses their train of thought mid-sentence." | Free | "Says 'Let me circle back to that.'" |

Name: _____

Date of meeting: _____

# Zoom Hog Bingo!

| | | | | |
|---|---|---|---|---|
| "Asks if this meeting is being recorded." | "Says 'I'll email you later about this.'" | "Talks to someone off-screen during the call." | "Claims they didn't get the agenda." | "Repeats the same question multiple times." |
| "Talks about lunch plans." | "Mentions how tired they are." | "Complains about their camera not working." | "Explains something already covered." | "Joins from their car." |
| "Interrupts to say 'Let me rephrase that.'" | "Mentions their bad internet connection." | "Shares their screen without warning." | Free | "Uses a distracting virtual background." |
| "Uses 'umm' excessively." | "Says 'This will only take a minute.'" | "Mentions how busy they are." | "Starts with 'This might be a stupid question, but...'" | "Talks over the host." |
| "Has loud background noise." | "Cracks an awkward joke that no one laughs at." | "Turns off their camera mid-meeting." | "Asks for a poll to be done." | "Overexplains their point." |

Name: _____

Date of meeting: _____

# Zoom Hog Bingo!

| | | | | |
|---|---|---|---|---|
| "Mentions their weekend plans." | "Says 'Just one more question.'" | "Suggests scheduling a follow-up meeting." | "Forgets to unmute before talking." | "Complains about technical difficulties." |
| "I know we're over time, but..." | Free | "Uses the word 'synergy' or 'circle back.'" | "Sorry, I didn't catch that—can you repeat it?" | "Thanks everyone at least three times." |
| "Let me just add one quick point." | "Talks about something unrelated to work." | "Asks for the slides or notes to be sent after the meeting." | "Repeats what someone else just said." | "Interrupts the speaker to make a point." |
| "Says 'Can everyone hear me?'" | "Joins late and asks to recap everything." | "Mentions their pet or child during the call." | "Asks a question unrelated to the topic." | "Talks over someone else." |
| "Goes on a long personal anecdote." | "Keeps their camera off and only chimes in to talk." | "Says 'I'll keep this brief' but doesn't." | "Can we circle back to what I said earlier?" | "Asks for clarification after it was explained." |

Name: _____

Date of meeting: _____

Printed in Great Britain
by Amazon